MW00932625

COVERED CALLS FOR BEGINNERS

A RISK-FREE WAY TO COLLECT "RENTAL INCOME"
EVERY SINGLE MONTH ON STOCKS YOU
ALREADY OWN

FREEMAN PUBLICATIONS

CONTENTS

HOW TO GET THE MOST OUT OF THIS BOOK

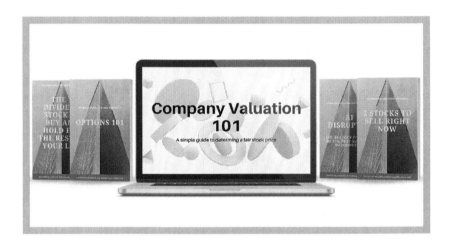

All of these bonuses are 100% free, with no strings attached. You don't need to enter any details except your email address.
To get your bonuses scan the QR code below or go to

https://freemanpublications.com/bonus

Or text the word BONUS to 844-968-4152 (US only)

Free bonus #1: Company Valuation 101 video course ($97 value)

In this 6 part video course you'll discover our process for accurately valuing a company. This will help you determine if a stock is overvalued, correctly valued or a bargain. Giving you an indicator whether to buy or not.

Free bonus #2: Guru Portfolios Analyzed ($37 value)

In these videos we analyze the stock portfolio's of Billionaire investors like Warren Buffett as well as top entre-preneurs like Bill Gates.

Free bonus #3: 4 "Backdoor" Ways to Profit from Cryptocurrency ($47 value)

When you have a paradigm-shifting technology like cryptocurrency and blockchain … there are multiple ways to profit from it.

But before you rush out and buy every altcoin under the sun… there is a smarter way of doing this.

The ways used by hedge funds and Billionaire investors to make massive profits from the price of Bitcoin and other cryptocurrencies.

And you don't need anything more than a regular brokerage account to do so. We covered exactly how to do this in a private call for our premium members recently and you'll get access to this video for free.

Free bonus #4: 2 Stocks to Sell Right Now ($17 value)

These 2 stocks are in danger of plummeting in the next 12 months. They're both popular with retail investors, and one is even in the top 5 most held stocks on Robinhood. Believe us; you don't want to be holding these going into 2021 and beyond.

Free bonus #5: AI Disruptor - The $4 Stock Poised to be the Next Big Thing in Computing ($17 value)

This under the radar company, which less than 1% of investors have heard of, is at the forefront of a breakthrough technology which will change our lives as we know them. Soon this technology will be in every smartphone, tablet and laptop on the planet.

Free bonus #6: Options 101 ($17 Value)

Options don't have to be risky. In fact, they were invented to *reduce* risk. It's no wonder that smart investors like Warren Buffett regularly use options to supplement their own long-term portfolio. In this quickstart guide we show you how options work, and why they're a tool to be utilized rather than feared.

Free bonus #7: The 1 Dividend Stock to Buy and Hold for the Rest of Your Life ($17 Value)

Dividends are the lifeblood of any income investor, and this stock is a cornerstone of any dividend strategy. A true dividend aristocrat with consistent payouts for over 50 years which you'll want to add to your portfolio for sure.

Free bonus #8: Top 3 Growth Stocks for 2022 ($17 Value)

Our 2020 selections outperformed the S&P 500 by 154%. Now we've released our 3 top picks for 2022.

To get your bonuses scan the QR code below or go to
https://freemanpublications.com/bonus

Or text the word BONUS to 844-968-4152 (US only)

2020: A CHAOTIC YEAR - HOW WE GOT TO THIS POINT

Wow. What a year 2020 has been. We went from the stock market hitting record highs to having the largest single week decline since the 2008 Financial Crisis. Then within six months, we were back to the previous highs again.

However, this year was just part of a larger period of unprecedented economic activity. While the stock market saw one of its best decades ever after the lows we experienced after the 2008 financial crisis. Economic recovery has hinged on something that is almost artificial.

Governments initially began printing money in the form Quantative Easing to prevent the entire financial ecosystem from collapsing. They quickly got used to the habit though and now printing money is second nature to them. Another monetary policy they've adhered to is rock-bottom interest rates. The theory behind this being that with interest rates so low, consumers will be less fearful of borrowing cash to fund purchases. This in turn will kickstart the economy.

That's the theory anyway. In practice, results have varied. While American economic activity increased, the likes of Japan never truly recovered. The Japanese economy has grown at a fixed rate of 1.14%

(well below other developed nations) since 1986, and interest rates have been at an all time low throughout this time. However, the recent pandemic has wiped out even those meager gains, and the economy has fallen back to the same level it held in 2008.

For an investor, this environment has been a tricky one to navigate. Buying an index fund that tracks the S&P 500 would have been a profitable investment. On the flip side though, we have the specter of increased inflation thanks to relentless money printing.

There is also the fact that rock-bottom interest rates don't provide any safe sources of income. In the past, savings accounts and certificates of deposit provided some degree of investment return that allowed you to stay ahead of inflation.

This isn't the case anymore. Inflation is currently hovering at around one percent but is projected to increase to around two percent (Ferreira, 2019). In 1999, the average return for a 1 year bank CD was 4.85%. Today that same 1 year CD pays just 0.46%, which doesn't even allow you to keep up with inflation.

At this point, savings accounts aren't really savings accounts; they're more like depletion accounts as inflation eats away at the real value of your money.

In such an environment, alternative investments have gained popularity. Gold and silver prices have surged thanks to the steady devaluation that paper money printing has caused. Cryptocurrencies have risen in popularity to the point where they're a bona fide alternative investment class.

Even the likes of hedge fund managers such as Paul Tudor Jones have dedicated portions of their portfolio to invest in cryptocurrencies (Schatzker, 2020). The central idea behind all of these investments is that they're a hedge against the devaluation of paper money.

But as attractive as they may be, none of these alternatives address the real issue - the possibility of utilizing cash flow to overcome inflation.

CAPITAL GAINS AND CASH FLOW

Traditionally, we as investors tend to think of our stock market investments in terms of capital gains. We buy a stock hoping that it will rise in price in the future, which will make us money.

While capital gains are undoubtedly the primary drivers of profit in the market, by solely focusing on capital gains, we ignore another source of investment profits: cash flow.

Cash flow provides us with the opportunity to leverage our investments for free. Consider the way a traditional dividend reinvestment plan works. We get paid to buy more stock or units of whatever is paying them the dividend.

Real estate investors understand the value of cash flow, but stock market investors tend to overlook this. Stock investors rely solely on capital gains and end up focusing on gains that are mostly unrealized. Unrealized meaning that you only receive cash when you sell your investment.

The smart thing to do is to receive cash flow from your investments. If you receive enough cash, you can overcome the relatively low inflation rates that currently exist. Doing this also gives you more options (no pun intended). You can reinvest into the same instrument or you can use the cash to power other investments.

This is the same strategy that Warren Buffett used to power the initial growth of his investment vehicle, Berkshire Hathaway (Schroeder, 2009). Buffett would buy companies that produced huge amounts of free cash flow and use the cash to buy even more cash producing companies.

This is why he has always favored the insurance industry since these companies produce loads of free cash flow thanks to excess premiums, known as *float*. By doing this, Buffett managed to leverage his initial investment across multiple companies. While you, as an individual investor, can't buy entire companies in this way, you can use the same underlying strategy to put extra money into your brokerage account each month.

There's a problem that investors will face, however. The cash flow that you receive in the form of dividends comes at a cost. Every company grows over the long term, at the rate at which its earnings grow. By paying dividends, the company is choosing a lower growth rate. Companies that pay dividends also tend to be mature and well past the growth stage.

So what should an investor do? Do you have to choose between capital gains and cash flow? This is where our solution comes into the picture.

FREEMAN COVERED CALL RULE #1

THE BEST INVESTOR'S AIM TO GET BOTH CAPITAL GAINS AND INCOME FROM THEIR PORTFOLIO

USING COVERED CALLS FOR INCOME

The covered call strategy involves writing or selling options. It is a safe and straightforward way to generate steady cash flow every month. It does not hamper your long-term capital gains in any way, so you get the best of both worlds. More importantly, the covered call is entirely safe if executed correctly, and contains no additional risk than just owning stock.

You might be thinking that since it involves options, it's guaranteed to be tricky to execute. You're not alone in thinking this way. Most long-term investors avoid options like the plague because of their perceived complexity. While it's true that options can be complicated, the fact is that you can choose the degree of complexity you want to implement when using them.

Contrary to popular opinion, options are often used by famous long-term buy and hold investors such as Warren Buffett and Bill Ackman. Ackman's firm Pershing Square Capital Management recently made over two billion dollars with options designed to profit from the fall of the markets following the COVID-19 crisis (Nagarajan, 2020). While Ackman's shorts involved the use of complex derivatives, they were essentially options trades. Buffett has famously written puts (a type of option that you'll learn all about shortly) as a means of generating cash flow to invest in other activities (*Case Study - Warren Buffett Writing Put Options To Obtain A Lower Stock Purchase Price*, 2019).

Covered calls are one of the simplest options strategies you can employ. They require you to understand a few basics about options, but you don't need any special market access or even a margin account to execute them. Most brokers will allow you to write covered calls with a standard cash account.

This means you don't need to worry about maintaining a higher account equity balance or even worry about violating the pattern day trader (PDT) rule. You won't incur higher commissions or trading costs. In short, covered calls are as much of an investment strategy as buying and holding stock.

You do have to start somewhere, though. You need to learn the basics of how options work and how they help you generate steady gains in the market. This book is going to walk you through every single step of the covered call strategy. We've just said that it's simple and easy to understand, but this doesn't mean we're going to cover it cursorily and then leave you to it.

We're going to take you on a deep tour of why covered calls are so powerful and how you can benefit from implementing them. Best of all, you'll be making consistent monthly cash flow with this strategy in addition to accumulating capital gains with your buy and hold investments.

Covered calls should be a part of your portfolio since the cash they generate will allow you to invest in growth-oriented strategies, or you can utilize them for any other purpose. Leveraging your investments without debt is a powerful way of increasing your wealth. Covered calls allow you to do exactly that.

There are no complex technical analysis charts in this book. The few illustrations that are here are simple and easy to understand. You don't need to learn fancy chart patterns or any other geometrical shapes that somehow reveal the market's intentions. Truth be told, most of those techniques don't work as well as they claim.

Instead, you'll learn how you can identify simple cues that make writing covered calls a viable strategy. The best part is that once you implement them, you'll make money even if the market does nothing, which, as we'll explain later in this book, is its default state.

We've made some assumptions when writing this book. We've assumed that you already have investment experience and have an active brokerage account where you hold your investments. If you understand the basics of how the stock market works, this book will pose no challenge to you.

We also hope that you are curious about using options as an alternative asset class to generate cash flow and gains. For this reason, we'll begin this book by first explaining how options work and the terminology associated with them. So without further ado, let's dive into the world of options!

1

OPTIONS 101 – FROM OLIVE PRESSES TO WARREN BUFFETT

W hat are options, and how do they work? Are they really complicated securities that you should stay away from as a levelheaded investor?

Options are an instrument that have been used since ancient times. In fact, their usage predates even the stock market.

The term "options contracts" is a relatively new term when considering how long they've been in use. This name was given to them once the stock market started to gain popularity. However, in a business sense, they've existed in one form or another for thousands of years.

If you're a follower of philosophy, you'll probably recognize the name Thales of Miletus. In case you aren't, Thales was the founder of the Stoic philosophical school of thought, which began in ancient Greece. Thales became famous by standing in a public arena (known as a stoa) and voicing his thoughts and opinions.

Thales was an intelligent man, and one of his passions was the weather and climate around ancient Greece. He reasoned that the climate was a part of the universe, and since man was also a part of the universe, man must take the time to understand the weather.

One of his most notable breakthroughs was in his understanding of solar and lunar cycles. In fact, he is believed to be the first person to predict a solar eclipse successfully. However, because Thales was not a wealthy man, societal elites ridiculed him. Although his ideas were revolutionary, they lacked practical application.

So Thales put his knowledge of the climate to use by predicting future olive harvests. He predicted these and also had "skin in the game" because he used a very similar tool to a modern-day options contract to profit from the harvests.

THALES' OLIVE PRESS CONTRACTS

Thanks to his meteorological bent, Thales managed to figure out that weather patterns indicated favorable conditions for the upcoming olive harvest. The olive harvest was the largest event in Thales' home-town of Miletus. Olive farmers and olive oil traders flocked to the town in the hopes of realizing a profit.

As with any farming endeavor, understanding weather patterns gave a person in these markets an edge. Thales had an edge, but he also had a problem. He was broke. So he needed to find a way to take advantage of his insight without putting up too much money.

He hit upon an ingenious plan. The concept of buying usage rights to the olive presses (which were used to turn olives into olive oil) was common in ancient Greece. The idea was that any person could approach an olive press owner and pay a small amount to obtain first usage rights to the press.

These rights would be valid for a certain period of time as negotiated by the buyer and the press owner. The buyer of the rights would pay the seller a small amount as a token of good faith. This system made sense for the olive press owners since they were guaranteed a payment. The rights holder acted as a salesman and brought olive farmers and traders to them without the press owner having to worry about finding customers.

The rights holder, in turn could then sell these rights to someone else and collect a profit on the amount they paid to acquire said rights. Thales planned to use these rights to turn his meager savings into a fortune. He went around buying the first-use rights to every press in Miletus. There are no official records that mention how much he spent, but one imagines he went all-in on his investment.

His prediction about the weather was right, and there was a bumper olive harvest. Farmers and merchants flocked to Miletus to process their olives and discovered that some guy named Thales owned the usage rights to all the presses in town. Thales sold these rights to merchants and gained far more than what he originally paid for them. After that, he lived out the rest of his days as a now wealthy philosopher.

Lessons Learned

There are certain aspects of Thales' deal that we would like to draw your attention to. First, note that the cost of these rights was far lower than the cost of buying an olive press outright. Thales could have purchased a few presses and competed against other olive press owners. Given the bumper crop, he would have made some money, and it would have been a solid investment.

However, it wasn't the best choice in terms of potential profit. For the same amount of money that would have bought him several presses, he managed to corner the olive press market by purchasing the rights to use all the presses in town. These rights therefore enabled him to leverage his investment massively. His risk was limited to what he invested in the purchase of the rights.

A common problem with utilizing debt-based leverage is that you can lose more than what you invest. This wasn't the case here. Thales put himself in a position to multiply his investment and earn a huge profit without exposing himself to any additional risk above what he had initially invested.

Lastly, note that the press merchant kept the money earned from the usage rights, no matter what. Thales could not ask for a refund. Also, the person who bought the usage rights from Thales still had to pay the press owner money to use the machine. The right only granted them access to it and not the right to use it for free. Thus, the merchants had no risk in the deal, aside from Thales not being able to draw in anyone. This was mitigated by the bumper harvest of course.

Thales' mechanism had all the hallmarks of a modern *call* option contract.

- **The Option:** Thales bought the rights, but not the obligation to use the olive presses
- **The Expiry Date:** These rights expired on a specific date
- **The Ability to Trade the Option**: He could keep these rights for himself, or he could sell them to another buyer
- **The Premium:** Thales paid for his rights upfront, and this amount stayed the same no matter the eventual state of the harvest

Keep these points in mind as you read on. Leaving ancient Greece, we now travel to Holland in the 17th century. This episode will highlight another aspect of options contracts that will be useful for you to understand.

TULIP MANIA

By the 17th century, the industrial revolution had seized control of Europe, and the continent's financial markets were booming. These markets had also acquired the sophistication of modern markets in terms of instruments available to trade. The average Dutch citizen was as aware of the stock market as the average American is today (*History of Options Trading - How Options Came About*, 2017).

This is to say they were aware of the money-making possibilities but were prone to making bad choices due to a lack of investment education. Dutch merchants visited far-flung corners of the globe and brought back all sorts of luxuries with them. One such luxury was the humble tulip.

The Netherlands is famous for its tulips these days, but back then, tulips were an exotic flower. No one in continental Europe had grown them, and the Hapsburgs of Austria were one of the few royal families who even had access to these flowers. They grew primarily in Ottoman-ruled Turkey and this infused them with an even more exotic aura.

As prosperity grew in Dutch society, ownership of tulips became a status symbol. It's hard to equate this fervor with anything in modern times since many things are viewed as desirable these days. Perhaps diamonds come the closest. However, in that time, with very few outlets for distraction and newfound prosperity, the fervor for tulips was probably a thousand times stronger than it is for diamonds these days.

The tulip mania as it's called these days began slowly. First, the prices of tulips began to rise. Dutch farmers noticed this and began growing tulips instead of boring stuff like wheat. These farmers brought their flowers to the market and noticed that tulip prices were significantly higher in cities than in the countryside.

There were simply more wealthy people in the cities, after all. Within cities such as Amsterdam, tulip connoisseurs were springing up every day. The various varieties of tulips were dissected and soon a tulip wasn't just a tulip. Different types were given different levels of status. Similar to how different varieties and vintages of wine can sell for upwards of $10,000 a bottle.

Farmers began flooding the markets with their tulips, and the demand kept increasing as more people became wealthy and wanted access to them. The less prosperous sections of society recognized that tulips seemed to be in favor for some reason. Everyone was buying them, so even those without means dipped into their savings and bought tulips as well. Demand began to grow exponentially, and soon Dutch farmers could not keep up with it. After all, no one can make a tulip grow faster, and people wanted their tulips right away! Which is why importing tulips from Turkey wasn't possible due to the long transit time, because overland routes were still the primary means of transport - combined with the tulips being subject to theft from bandits along the way. As a result, demand outpaced supply and prices rose exponentially. The prices of tulips, which began at the equivalent of a few modern dollars, rose as high as the price of a house!

With euphoria firmly in control, everyone wanted in on the action. The person who had bought one tulip cursed themselves for not having bought two. The person with 100 wanted 200. Soon, the existing owners of tulips spotted an opportunity. Much like how Thales bought the rights to use the olive presses, tulip owners began selling rights to buy or sell their tulips.

These rights traded for high prices thanks to insatiable demand. As the tulip supply remained exactly the same, the prices of these options increased dramatically and became almost equal to that of a tulip itself. People offered their homes as collateral in exchange for the right to buy a tulip. They then sold these rights for even higher prices to someone else and so on.

At some point, sellers of these rights could not find new buyers. The prices were simply too high, and so they began decreasing. As prices began decreasing, people realized that they were trading a pretty ordinary-looking flower. The rich had moved on and found other pleasures since tulips were now a dime a dozen. It was as if everyone woke up at the same time.

Exact records are hard to find, but by all accounts, the prices of the humble tulip fell right back to where they began. People who had pledged their homes as collateral were out on the streets. Almost everyone lost money, and as a result, the Dutch economy collapsed.

Some sources argue the Dutch never regained their financial footing thanks to this event and would eventually lose out to the British and French in the race to colonize the world (Mackay, 2014).

Points To Consider

The colonial ramifications of this episode aside, here are a few points you need to understand that relate to present-day options. First, the options traded on tulip ownership were almost exactly the same as modern options that trade on stock ownership. The features that we pointed out in the example of Thales' trade existed here as well.

However, the big difference is that while Thales' bet is an example of intelligent investment, the tulip incident is an example of unintelligent speculation. The option to buy a tulip is just a tool. It wasn't the options' fault that tulips themselves were worthless or that their demand at the time was shaky.

If a speculator risks too much while buying options, they will lose a lot of money. Options in this scenario were used as speculative tools, and this is what created the problem in the first place.

Notice that Thales' bet was based on sound principles. Sure, it was based on the weather, but the man was investing in the probability of there being a good harvest of olives. He tied his investment to something tangible. The people of 17th century Holland were not.

Options are just a tool, not a get-rich-quick scheme. They tend to attract the label of being risky thanks to the way in which people use them. They can be misused just as stock investments can be. This misuse is why options trading was banned in London and Japan at the same time when tulip mania was unfolding. In fact, as the world moved into the 19th century, America was one of the few places where options could be traded.

MODERN OPTIONS CONTRACTS

The boom in options trading in America began in the late 1800s when Russell Sage created an over-the-counter market for them. Sage used the options he sold to take control of entire companies in the railroad industry. He eventually lost his money as the authorities began cracking down on such behavior.

Another famous speculator who used options was Jesse Livermore. Livermore used options unknowingly during his initial days when he would trade in bucket shops. Bucket shops no longer exist but were a fixture of the stock market in the late 19th Century. You can think of them as mini black market stock exchanges, where anyone could buy or sell shares. These establishments would often offer their customers money on margin, often at ridiculous levels like 100:1 (where $1 could be used to trade up to $100 worth of shares). The shops would then "bucket" their customers' orders together and then trade against them, reasoning that most of their customers were wrong about the markets. This is completely illegal today, but stock trading was far less regulated in Livermore's day than it is now.

Once Livermore became wealthy, he would use options to help manipulate the prices of a company's stock. The Securities and Exchange Commission (SEC) was formed partly due to such activities, and Livermore's trading days ended with a whimper.

The advent of the SEC ensured that the securities markets lost their Wild West nature. Laws were put in place and these have evolved to the point where the markets these days are completely transparent. The stock market is intensely regulated, and investors can place their money knowing that the authorities are on the job.

Most options contracts these days are available on stocks. There are options available on forex instruments and even on bonds and interest rate instruments. However, these are usually available only to institutional traders and investors. From a retail investor's perspective, stock options are the most commonly available ones.

A major advantage of options trading is that unlike buy and hold investing, in which you only profit when a stock moves up. Options allow you to profit regardless of if the stock moves up or down, or even if it moves laterally and stays at the same price.

There are two kinds of options that will be available to you. The first is a call option. Call options, or *calls* as they're known, give the buyer the right (but not the obligation) to buy the underlying stock at an agreed price - before a certain date. If you choose to not buy the underlying stock, this is perfectly fine.

Thales' first-use rights were effectively a call option. He was betting on the fact that the desirability of those olive presses would increase. Similarly, buyers of calls bet on the fact that the price of the underlying will increase. Call options buyers make money only when the price of the underlying increases. This is irrespective of whether the underlying is a stock, bond or anything else.

The second kind of option is a *put*. Puts give you the option to sell the underlying. Just as with calls, you have the option but not the obligation to sell the underlying. Note that you still buy a put despite it giving you the power to sell the underlying stock. You're obtaining the option to short a stock without going on margin.

There are many other kinds of options that are available to institutional investors, but these two are more than enough for you to make money with. When used in a smart manner, you can use options to not only provide you with a solid monthly cash flow, you can also use them to *reduce* your risk.

Where They Trade

Like stocks, options have their own exchange. This is the Chicago Board Options Exchange or CBOE. The CBOE was founded in 1973 and brought options trading to the modern world by taking it off the over-the-counter (OTC) markets. OTC markets still exist for options, but the ones you'll see on your broker's software will be traded on the CBOE.

Like stocks, options have a price spread. In case you're unfamiliar with it, the price spread identifies the buying and selling price of a particular instrument. The price at which you buy an instrument is the *ask* or *offer* price. The price at which you can sell it is the *bid*. Options spreads depend on the liquidity available in the market and on the volatility of the stock itself.

The more volatile a stock is, the larger the options price spread will be. The price of an options contract is called a *premium*. This is because options often function as insurance against adverse market moves. This is why some insurance-related terms are connected to them.

Like stocks, calls and puts can be bought or shorted. Shorting an option tends to confuse many first-time investors. After all, if you want to bet on the price of a stock declining, you could simply buy a put. Why would anyone want to short a call? The answer is that options allow you to make non-directional bets.

When you buy a put, you're explicitly stating your opinion that the price of the stock (underlying) is going to fall. You'll profit only if the price falls. If it moves sideways, you won't make money.

However, by selling a call, you're stating your opinion that the stock price will not rise. This is different from saying you're betting on a fall. Saying something will not rise is to say that it might move sideways *or* it might go down. Selling a call gives you the ability to profit no matter what happens. This highlights one of the huge advantages of options. They give you the ability to profit even in sideways markets.

Below are some of the other advantages.

. . .

Superior Cash Flow Opportunities

Options contracts allow you to leverage your investment. They do this in two ways. The first is in the way they're structured. Each options contract covers 100 shares of the underlying stock. Options premiums are usually a fraction of the price of the individual shares so you can control 100 shares by paying a much smaller amount.

For example, to purchase 100 shares of the exercise equipment company Peloton, which currently trades around $80, you would need to pay $8,000. However, if you purchased one $20 call option (with each contract representing 100 shares), your total outlay would be only $2,000 (1 contracts representing 100 shares * $20 market price). Giving you $6,000 to invest elsewhere.

Calculating options contract prices is a separate topic that we'll explain in the next chapter. Briefly, the price of a contract depends on how long it has until it expires and on the current market price. Calculating this isn't essential for your trading, so it isn't as if you need to calculate prices all the time. It's just good information to know.

The second way in which leverage is created is by using options to generate cash flow. As we mentioned in the introduction, covered calls are a strategy that create this kind of situation.

Non-Directional Trading

Where options truly shine is when it comes to implementing non-directional trading strategies. You've seen just one example of this in the previous section where you can take advantage of stock prices that either fall or move sideways with one options position. Options also allow you to take advantage of situations with unpredictable prices movements.

For example, if you have a situation in a stock where prices will either fall or rise massively, options trading strategies can help you set up a trade where you don't care about the direction in which the prices move, just the degree with which they move. These strategies are called *Volatility Trading Strategies.*

In stock trading, volatility refers to the degree and force with which the price of an instrument moves. If a stock jumps around all the time, it's far more volatile than a stock that moves steadily without too many surprises.

Investors in the stock market treat volatility as a known unknown. They may not know in which direction prices will move, but they can say with a degree of certainty that there will be a significant move in one or both directions. It can help them or hurt them, and since they don't have a way of taking advantage of it, they simply hold onto their investments through it.

Options traders, however, can target some obvious scenarios where volatility will be present in the market. For example, an important economic announcement such as an increase or decrease in interest rates will produce massive market volatility. You might not know which way the market will move, but you do know that volatility will increase. Certain options strategies allow you to target the increase or decrease in volatility.

Another major advantage of options trading and investment is that they allow you to define your risk with pinpoint accuracy. Let's say you've bought shares of a company at $100. Theoretically, your maximum risk is realized if the price of the stock falls to zero.

Many investors utilize stop loss orders to cap their risk. They place a stop loss order at $50. This theoretically limits their risk to $50 per share. However, stop loss orders are not infallible due to liquidity and volatility. In extreme market conditions, prices jump stop loss orders and investors receive prices that are far worse than intended.

In our scenario above, if the price spread skips past $50 (like if bid prices move from $51 straight to $40 due to a lack of liquidity) then you will receive a sale price of $40, which increases your risk to $60 per share.

This situation does not exist with options. You can fix a certain price and that price will be honored no matter what. You'll learn how this works in the next chapter when we detail the specifics of an options contract.

While these advantages are very real, it would be a disservice to you if we didn't discuss some disadvantages you ought to be aware of before trading options.

Improper Use of Leverage

Options provide you with the ability to leverage your money, and this can create problems. There is nothing stopping you from risking more money than you can afford.

This feature of options tends to attract a specific type of market participant. This person is often interested in get-rich-quick schemes and tends to overleverage themselves. As a result, they lose money and options receive a reputation of being risky. Options help you fix a maximum risk limit accurately, but you still need to understand how to use them correctly. They aren't, however, a magic bullet that will eliminate losses.

Another temptation with options is to overcomplicate them. We refer to complexity as being something that you don't understand. There are options strategies that involve many moving parts. If you don't understand these parts of the strategy's nuances, you will more than likely end up making a loss.

This is why we believe that beginners should stick to simple options strategies, such as writing covered calls. These strategies have very few things to keep track of, and they don't require much maintenance. In fact, later on in the book we outline 3 simple rule-based strategies for managing your trades without needing to stare at stock charts all day.

FREEMAN COVERED CALL RULE #2

YOU CAN MAKE A STEADY MONTHLY INCOME BY ONLY USING BASIC OPTIONS STRATEGIES

Time Decay

One disadvantage that will hurt you if you ignore it is the phenomenon of time decay. We'll explain this in great detail in the next chapter. Briefly, time decay refers to the event where option premiums (prices) decrease over time. If you're buying an options contract, then time decay means an ill-timed purchase could make capturing gains very difficult.

However, by selling options, which is what you'll be doing with covered calls, you actually use time decay to your advantage.

Now that you have a clearer picture of what the advantages and disadvantages are of trading options, it's time to dive deeper into them and take a look at how these contracts are structured.

2

THE BASICS OF OPTIONS CONTRACTS AND OPTIONS TERMINOLOGY

One of the reasons understanding options can be tricky is that they come with a lot of terms and phrases that scare away ordinary investors. Investing in stocks is pretty straightforward. There's no jargon involved, or at least not so much so that it makes the entire endeavor intimidating.

Options terminology revolves around the way a contract is structured. Once you understand how the structure works, you'll have no problems grasping what the various terms mean. You've already learned that you'll have access to two kinds of options: Calls and puts. Let's look at each of these contracts separately and understand how the terms and conditions associated with them work.

CALL OPTIONS

A call option gives you the right to buy the underlying security at a certain price. Here's how it works. The underlying security is typically a stock. Your broker will provide you with access to various calls that you can buy on this stock. All of these calls will have different strike prices.

An option's strike price is the level at which it will make you money. For example, let's say you decided to buy a call on Amazon stock. Amazon shares are currently trading at $3,100. If you buy a call with a strike price of $3,000, you can immediately use it to make money on the stock. However, this isn't profitable because you have paid a premium for the option contract, which will not offset the gains from the stock itself.

A call with a strike price of $4,000 cannot be used just yet to make money. The price of the underlying stock (Amazon) has to move past the $4,000 mark first. Choosing the right strike price is very important with a call or a put because it determines how far the underlying has to move in order for you to start making money.

For example, let's say Amazon moves past $4,000 to $4,500. In this scenario, you've earned a profit of $500. You can use your call to buy Amazon at the fixed price of $4,000 and then sell it back to the market at the current price of $4,500. This is why investors buy calls when they're bullish about a stock's prospects.

How do you use a call to buy the underlying? This is as simple as clicking a button in your broker's software. The process is called exercising your option. If you have the money required to buy the requisite number of shares of the underlying stock, your broker will buy them for you and debit the cash from your account.

Remember that each call options contract covers 100 shares of the underlying. This means if you exercise a single call options contract of Amazon at $4,000 you'll need to pay $400,000 (4000*100) in cash from your account. Over and above this, you'll also need to pay the premium when you buy the call.

The premium is not recoverable under any circumstances. Whether your trade goes for a profit or a loss, you will lose this money. Therefore, when exercising or selling a call, you need to make sure you earn at least this much back in order to break even. This is why you can't just buy calls for options which are lower than the current stock price and exercise them immediately.

Looking at the example of Amazon, you might be thinking that $400,000 is a pretty steep price to pay. What if you don't have that much cash? Does this mean you can't trade the options of high price stocks? Not quite. The option's premium fluctuates as well depending on how close the underlying market price is to the strike price.

The closer the strike price comes to making you money on the contract, the higher it rises in value. For example, if the underlying price is $100, the call option with a strike price of $101 will be priced higher than the option with a strike price of $105. This is because the 101 call is more likely to make you money since the underlying is closer to it and therefore, will be priced higher.

An option's premium has two portions to it: The intrinsic value and the time value (also known as extrinsic value). In order to understand how these work, you first need to understand expiry dates.

Expiry Dates

All options contracts have an expiry date attached to them. This means that whether you want to exercise or sell the option, you need to do that before the expiry date. Typically options are available with expiration dates in the current month, the next month and the month after that, although many larger stocks now have weekly options as well. There are also special options known as LEAPs, which expire more than six months in the future.

Different stocks have different monthly cycles that govern when their options are available to trade. All you need to do is look at your broker's software and that will display all the options contracts available to trade, as well as the number of days until that particular contract expires.

Let's consider an example. Amazon stock is selling for $3,100. You can buy two calls: one with a strike price of $3,000 and another with a strike price of $2,600. Both of these calls expire in the same month, which is 30 days away. Their premium will differ since clearly, they're not worth the same.

The 2600 call will make you more money. Its price will be a sum of its intrinsic value and its time value. The intrinsic value is a straightforward mathematical calculation. It's simply the difference between the underlying price and the strike price. In the case of the 2600 call, it's calculated as:

Intrinsic value of 2600 AMZN call = $3,100 - $2,600 = $500

In the case of the 3000 call, the intrinsic value will be:

Intrinsic value of 3000 AMZN call = $3,100 - $3,000 = $100

This leaves us with the time value. Unlike the intrinsic value, the time value is not a straightforward mathematical calculation.

Here's how it works. The longer an option has until expiration, the more valuable it is. The reasoning is that there is more time for the underlying to move into a position where the option can make you money.

The closer it is to expiry, the less value it has, since there is less time for the option to make you money. Time value is a constantly changing thing and there is no straightforward method of calculating it. The people who figured out a model to accurately calculate the value of an option by taking time value into account won a Nobel Prize for it. That should give you an idea of the complexity.

But don't let this put you off. The concept of time value is far more important for you to understand than calculating the value itself. Specifically, you need to understand that time value decreases as the option approaches expiry.

This phenomenon is called time decay. Time decay usually accelerates once the option is less than 30 days away from expiry. This means the price of the option will decline faster and will rise less forcefully in this period. This is irrespective of whether the option can make you money or not.

The expiry date can work in one of two ways. Some options can be exercised or sold only on the expiry date, these are called European options. The other type of options, called American options, can be exercised on any day leading up to the expiry date. As the majority of covered calls are written on American options, that is what we'll be focusing on in this book.

In and Out of the Money

In the case of a call option, the investor makes money only when the underlying price is greater than the option's strike price. If an option can make its owner money, it's said to be *in the money* or ITM. When the strike price equals the market price, the option is said to be *at the money* or ATM.

When the call option is *outside the money* or OTM, the strike price is greater than the market price. In this scenario, the option buyer would lose money if they exercised it. Remember how intrinsic value is calculated for a call? The strike price is subtracted from the underlying price.

However in the case of an OTM option, this would result in a negative value. For example, if Amazon is at $3,100 and if you buy a call with a strike price of $4,000, the intrinsic value is -$900. Options cannot have negative values. Therefore OTM options always have zero intrinsic value and have just their time value attached to them.

With OTM options, if the underlying price increases past the strike price turning the option ITM, the option premium value will rise accordingly since it will gain intrinsic value. Its time value will also increase by some amount despite moving closer to expiry since the probability of making money is taken into account in this value. It won't rise as quickly in the final 30 days as it would the rest of the time, but there will be some appreciation.

A Sample Options Trade

Let's say you've spotted a reason for Amazon to increase in value from its current price of $3,100. You think it's going to go past $4,000 over the next two months easily. Buying the stock is going to be expensive, so you decide to pull a Thales and buy calls (the right to buy Amazon) instead. After all, buying 1 options contract (which covers 100 shares) is a much smaller upfront investment than buying 100 shares of the stock.

Since you think a price target of $4,000 is probable, you'd want to pick a call with a strike price that is less than $4,000 but still leaves you with enough room to earn a profit.

You take a look at the calls available and decide that $3,500 is the right strike price. At this level, the option has no intrinsic value since it's OTM. If you choose an expiry date that is 60 days away, you'll give yourself enough room for the time value to increase once the underlying moves past the strike price.

Let's say this call costs you $50. You'll pay $5,000 upfront since every options contract controls 100 shares. Options prices are quoted on a per share basis, so you'll need to multiply their prices by 100 to figure out how much you need to pay. Once this is done, you sit back and wait.

As Amazon increases in price, your calls become more valuable. Eventually, with a week remaining until expiry, the underlying sells for $3,900. This results in a $400 gain in intrinsic value per share. However, your time value is quickly decreasing since there isn't much time left till expiry.

At this point, you have two choices. You could exercise the call and buy 100 shares of Amazon at your $3,500 strike price. Or you could simply sell the call (which is what Thales did) and earn a profit. Let's assume the time value declines to zero. This isn't a problem because the call still has an intrinsic value of $400 per share in it.

Selling the option will result in a credit of $40,000 to your account. You paid $5,000 to buy the call. This leaves you with a profit of $35,000. Pretty good for a couple months' work! However, this is the best-case scenario. If the price moves to, say, $3,501, you'll earn a far lower profit of $100.

The worst-case scenario for you would be the underlying not moving past your strike price of $3,500. What happens then? This condition illustrates why options are so great. Your contract will be worthless since it will be OTM upon expiry. You can simply let it expire and do nothing. All you'll lose is your initial $5,000 investment, which is how much you paid to buy the call.

PUT OPTIONS

Call options give you the right to buy the stock at a particular price, whereas puts give you the right to sell the underlying at a particular price. You can choose to not exercise the put, of course, since you aren't obliged to do so. Puts tend to confuse new investors a bit since you're effectively shorting the underlying stock, which is not something you'd usually do with regular investing.

Going back to our example with Amazon, let's say you felt that it was due to fall from $3,100 to $2,000. You could short the stock, but this requires a margin account and you'll need to take care of maintenance and initial margin requirements.

Put options solve this problem. You don't need a margin account to buy puts as part of a basic strategy. We'll clarify this towards the end of this chapter. For now, let's look at how the sample trade with Amazon can work out.

Shorting Amazon with Options

The terminology associated with puts is the same as it is with calls. It's just that ITM and OTM conditions are flipped. Puts make you money when the underlying value is *less* than the strike price. This is when they're ITM. Puts are OTM when the price of the underlying is higher than the strike price.

For example, if Amazon is selling for $3,100, the 2,100 put is OTM, and the 3,500 put is ITM. In the case of a call, the 2,100 call will be ITM and the 3,500 call will be OTM. Always keep this in mind.

The calculation of intrinsic value is also flipped in the case of a put. A put gains intrinsic value when the underlying moves lower than the strike price. It has no intrinsic value as long as the underlying is greater than the strike price. The time value works in the same way as it does with a call.

Getting back to our example trade, you think the price of Amazon will decline to $2,000. Instead of shorting the stock, you buy puts with a strike price of $2,500. This is far enough away from the current market price to make the options cheap and is far enough away from the target price to give you a decent profit if the trade works out.

If Amazon declines to $2,000, you'll earn a profit of $500 per share or $50,000 per contract. If the put expires OTM you'll lose only the premium you paid for the put. Thus, the trade works pretty much the same way as it did in the case of a call.

We'd like to point out once again that you'll be buying the put, not shorting it. You can short or write a put, but that's not what's going on here. If you wish to benefit from a decline in prices, you buy a put. This is the equivalent to shorting the underlying without the hassle of having to borrow shares to do so.

BUYING AND WRITING OPTIONS

So far we've only dealt with scenarios that involve buying options, but we haven't considered the other side of the coin. Just as you can short stocks, you can sell options. Given the insurance-like function that options play, selling an option is also called writing an option. This is why you'll often see the covered call strategy referred to as "writing covered calls"

When you write an option, you're taking the other side of the trade. The buyer of the option has a choice of exercising it or not. The option writer, however, has no choice. They need to do whatever the buyer wants. If the buyer chooses to exercise the option, the writer/seller has to deliver.

This makes option writing a bit riskier than buying an option. The option buyer knows there is no obligation, but the option writer needs to construct their trade in such a way that they eliminate any risk.

Having said that, it isn't as if this risk cannot be managed. As you'll learn in the next chapter, with good risk management, you'll make *more* money with *less* risk writing options than buying them. In fact, covered calls are essentially risk-free, because writing the option itself doesn't increase your risk profile.

More on that later. For now, let's take a look at some sample scenarios so that you understand how writing an option works.

Writing a Put

This is something Warren Buffett has done in the past with Berkshire Hathaway. He has written puts on both Coca-Cola and the broad stock market index, the S&P 500 (SPX). Given his bullish bent, it makes sense why he'd follow this path. If he was convinced that the market or Coca-Cola's stock was going to rise, he'd take the bullish option.

Why did he write puts, though? Why not buy calls? This highlights an important difference between writing an option and buying one. When you buy an option, you're marrying yourself to the strike price. You need to be able to predict not just the strike price that will make you money but also the time it will take the underlying to move past that strike.

Most of us can't predict the next few minutes, let alone what will happen to a stock over the next few months. Writing a put allowed Buffett to divorce himself from the stock having to move past a particular strike price. Let's say Coca-Cola was selling at $40 and Buffett wrote puts at $20.

He's effectively saying that he believes the stock price will not fall below $20 over the expiry period of those puts. This is very different from saying the price will definitely rise past $50 (which is the case if he bought a call.) With a put option, even if Coca-Cola moves sideways and remains at $40, he makes money.

How does he make money? Remember that when you buy an option, you pay a premium. This premium is being paid to the option writer. Thus, if you write an option, you receive money from the option buyer, and you get to keep this cash no matter what. The put premium represents the maximum profit you will earn in the trade. The trade ends once the option expires.

When you write an option, the money is deposited into your account immediately. Therefore, writing an option is all about generating cash flow for yourself and keeping an eye out for the possibility of the option being exercised.

Therefore it is in your best interest for the option to expire worthless since you'll get to keep your premium.

FREEMAN COVERED CALL RULE #3

WHETHER YOU WRITE A PUT OR CALL OPTION, YOU ALWAYS GET PAID THE PREMIUM UPFRONT AND GET TO KEEP IT REGARDLESS OF WHETHER OR NOT THE OPTION FINISHES IN THE MONEY

But what happens if the option moves ITM and you're hit with an exercise from the option buyer? This process is called an assignment. If you're assigned an option, it means the buyer has exercised the option and you need to deliver. In the case of a put, the buyer is seeking to sell the stock. This means you'll have to buy the underlying at the strike price of the put. You'll have to hold onto these shares or sell it immediately for a loss; it's up to you.

For example, let's say the underlying price moves to $50 and you wrote a put for $55. Since his put is ITM, you are assigned it. You need to buy the stock for $55, which will be used by the put buyer to short the stock at that price.

You've just bought stock selling for $50 at $55. You can either hang onto the stock and hope for the market price to rise or you can sell immediately for a loss of five dollars per share and move on. Theoretically, writing a put exposes you to a small upside and a huge downside.

The price of a stock can go all the way to zero. This means your maximum risk on the trade is equal to the strike price of the put (strike price minus zero.) Your broker will require you to have a certain amount of cash in your account and you will also need to have a Level 3 options trading margin account. We'll explain these levels shortly.

Writing a put is therefore not something anyone can do. Generally speaking, writing puts is not a consistent way of making money and it isn't something you want to do if your aim is to earn steady cash flow.

Writing a Call

If writing a put is risky, writing calls is one of the riskiest things you can do. This is because the price of a stock can rise till infinity. In order to write a call, your broker will require you to have a Level 4 options trading margin account and will need to see proof of substantial experience. Even then, they might decline you these privileges.

But wait, isn't this entire book about writing calls? Why would we discuss a strategy which is so risky? Well the risk all has to do with the type of calls we are writing.

For now, let's look at what happens when you're assigned a call. Assuming you've convinced your broker to let you write a call, you'll earn the call premium upfront. You're now betting on the stock either declining or moving sideways. If you've been assigned the call, the worst has happened and the price has risen.

You'll now need to buy the underlying at the market price and sell it to the option buyer at the call's strike price. If the market price is $105 and the strike price is $90, you'll realize a loss of $15 per share. The risk in writing a call is that the price could rise to $200, $500 or even $1,000 before the buyer chooses to exercise it.

However, there is an easy way to eliminate the risk of writing a call. It's by already holding the stock you are writing calls against. This way, you profit both from the upside movement of the stock, and from the premium you received by writing the option. It's a win-win scenario and why the covered call is such a great options strategy.

TYPES OF OPTIONS TRADING ACCOUNTS

Different brokers have different ways of dealing with opening an options trading account. Most brokers classify options account types based on the type of strategies you can employ. There are four levels. The first level, Level 1, allows you to implement strategies where the maximum risk is defined. In order to trade covered calls, you need a Level 1 account. This is a pretty easy account to qualify for. Now, with many online brokers it's as simple as ticking a box when you open your stock trading account stating you would like the ability to trade options.

Your broker may also ask you if you need margin to trade. If you indicate that you do, you'll have to qualify for opening a margin account. Brokers usually require you to have a higher minimum balance to qualify for this. Covered calls don't require you to trade on margin, so you don't need this. Other strategies you can execute with a level 1 account are *cash secured puts*, which is writing an OTM put and having enough cash on hand to cover the assignment.

Level 2 accounts allow you to buy options. You can execute the strategies of the previous level, and you can buy puts and calls. This level's strategies don't require margin, but there is the possibility of loss that is undefined. This is why brokers consider these Level 2 strategies.

Level 3 and 4 accounts are reserved for complex strategies that require you to borrow on margin. Some brokers even have a Level 5 that is reserved for the riskiest strategies (from the broker's perspective, not necessarily from an execution perspective.)

The most important thing to know at this stage is that you can execute covered calls from a level 1 account, which is the easiest to get and will be available to any investor.

OPTION CHAINS

Another item you'll need to become familiar with is the option chain. While it may look complicated at first glance, it's quite simple once you get the hang of it. The option chain is just a visual representation of which options are available for you to buy or write at a particular time. Typically, the strike prices are listed in a column in the middle of the page. The call options are displayed to the left of the strike price, with the puts on the right.

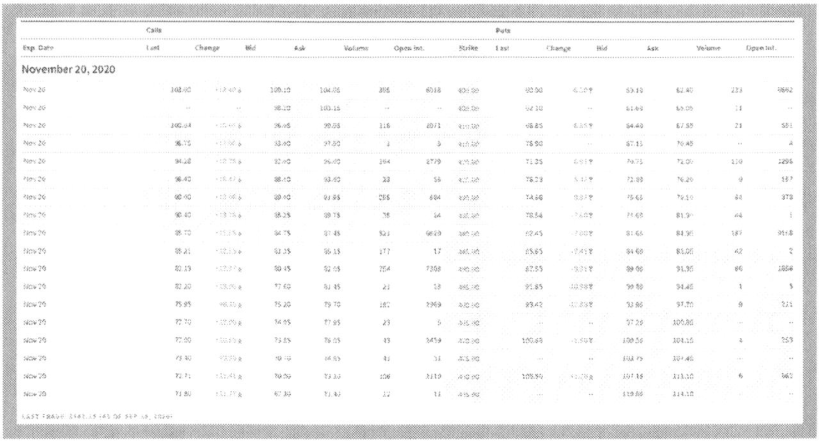

Figure 1: The options chain for Tesla stock (source: Nasdaq.com)

Brokers use color codes to indicate which options are ITM and which ones aren't. In figure 1, the shaded columns are ITM, and the white columns are OTM. Notice that the ITM call options are below the stock's current market price, whereas the ITM put options are above the current market price.

There will be a dropdown box on top that will indicate the expiry date of the options in the chain. In this case, the expiration date of the options (November 20th 2020) is listed on the left hand side.

The page will also list the bid and ask prices of each option at the different strike prices.

In addition to this, your brokerage platform may display other data, such as implied volatility, volumes and open interest. Volume is the same thing as with stocks, which is to say they indicate the number of contracts being traded. For example, in Figure 1, at the time the screenshot was taken, there were 177 call options contracts available at the 445 strike price. Remember, each contract represents 100 shares of stock.

On top of this, a typical option chain will display Implied volatility (not shown in figure 1) and open interest, which are option-specific terms.

Implied volatility or implied vol is denoted by the Greek letter sigma (Σ). It is expressed as a percentage or in terms of a standard deviation number and indicates how much the stock is likely to move in the near future. A higher implied volatility value indicates that the stock is going to be more volatile. You should also note that volatility is not directional, so higher volatility does not mean a stock will definitely move up or down. It is a measure of the amount it could move in *either* direction.

FREEMAN COVERED CALL RULE #4

IMPLIED VOLATILITY IS ALWAYS NON-DIRECTIONAL

Implied volatility should not be confused with historical volatility or beta. Beta indicates how volatile the stock has been in the past. Implied volatility is concerned with the near future. Also note the implied volatility can be divorced from the overall market volatility. The market's volatility is captured by the volatility index or VIX. Unless you are writing calls on indexes rather than stocks, your focus should be on implied volatility of that particular stock, rather than the VIX.

This brings to a close our look at how options contracts work and the terminology associated with them. As you can see, there are a lot of similarities present with options and stocks. For example, writing an option is the same as initiating a short position in it. It's just that the words used are different.

Now that you understand the terms, it's time to address the elephant in the room. Why have options acquired the reputation of being risky, and what are the things you should be aware of to mitigate these risks?

But before we get to that, as we've covered A LOT of ground in the past two chapters, here is a quick summary of everything we've learned so far:

- **Options** give the buyer the right, but not the obligation, to buy an asset at a specific price
- They have been around in one form or another for thousands of years and even predate the stock market
- You can use options if you think the price of an asset with rise, fall or stay the same
- A **call option** gives you the **right to buy** an asset at a fixed price
- A **put option** gives you the **right to sell** an asset at a fixed price
- The price you pay for an options contract is called the **premium**
- You pay the premium regardless of the outcome of the contract
- The price of the option premium is made up of two factors
- **Intrinsic value** - the difference between the price of the underlying and the how far the option is **in the money**
- If the option is **out of the money**, then the premium has no intrinsic value
- **Time value (or extrinsic value)** - the amount of time left in the options contract

- All options are fixed time contracts, which have a specific **expiry date**
- When you use your options contract to buy the asset at the agreed price, this is known as **exercising** the contract
- You must exercise the contract before the expiry date
- 1 options contract covers 100 shares of the underlying asset
- You can also **sell (or write)** options
- When you sell an options contract, you receive the premium upfront and get to keep it no matter what
- The **covered call** is a strategy which involves **selling call options on a stock you already own**
- You get paid the premium upfront, as well as benefitting if the price of your stock rises

And now, some questions to check that you've understood everything so far. Use the options chain in figure 1 for data. The answers are on the next page.

1. Using the bid price, how much would it cost you to buy 1 call options contract for Tesla at the 455 strike?

----

2. Using the ask price, how much would you receive if you sold 1 call options contract for Tesla at the 460 strike?

----

3. The options in figure 1 have 60 days to expiry. All other things being equal, would the price of these options be higher or lower in 30 days time?

----

4. Tesla traded at $442.50 when figure 1 was printed. The price of the call option at the 420 strike is $92. How much of this $92 is intrinsic value, and how much is time value?

ANSWERS FOR THE PREVIOUS QUESTIONS

1. At a bid price of $77.60, the price for 1 call option at the 455 strike would be $7,660. Remember, each options contract represents 100 shares of the underlying. So you need to multiply the bid price by 100 to find the price you will pay.

2. At the ask price of $79.70, if you sold 1 call option at the 460 strike you would receive a credit of $7,970 into your account. Selling options works the same way as buying them, in that each contract represents 100 shares of the underlying.

3. All other things being equal, we would expect option prices to **decline** in 30 days because options are an asset that decreases in value over time.

4. If Tesla is trading at $442.50, and the price of the 420 call option is $92. This $92 consists of $22.50 of intrinsic value, which is the difference between the price of the underlying and the strike price (442.50 – 420). The remaining $69.50 is therefore time value.

Remember, only ITM options have intrinsic value, because intrinsic value cannot be negative. OTM options only consist of time value.

3

MISUNDERSTANDINGS REGARDING OPTIONS

Options are misunderstood instruments in that they are often mischaracterized as being risky even by the most experienced investors. This depiction harms many investors because they incur massive opportunity costs by choosing to stay on the sidelines when it comes to options.

We're not suggesting you start trading options full time. What we recommend you do instead is use options as a part of your overall investment strategy. You can use options, particularly covered calls, to generate a safe return for yourself without exposing your account to additional risk.

As we mentioned earlier, many investors rely solely on capital gains from their investments. This is a mistake. It's a bit like buying a piece of property and letting it sit there in the hope that it'll increase in value over time. Smart property investors monetize their investment immediately by renting it. This gives them cash flow every month and they earn money from both the cash flow as well as capital gains. It's quite obvious for real estate investors to do this. However, many stock market investors don't follow this basic principle.

Instead of looking to generate cash flow, they seek more complicated ways of hedging their investments by investing in gold and silver. Some even stray into alternative assets like cryptocurrency. These may bring you capital gains, but they do nothing to provide additional cash flow.

Before we dive deeper into options as an investment tool, we must examine the difference between investment and speculation. Examining the differences will help you understand why options trading is a good move for your portfolio and why so many traders mischaracterize these instruments.

INVESTMENT AND SPECULATION

Benjamin Graham was one of the first people to tackle the question of investment versus speculation in his book *The Intelligent Investor* (Graham, 1949). Graham famously suffered through the Great Depression, resulting in him adopting an extremely conservative view of the market. This is not to say that conservative views are wrong. If anything, Graham's views were necessary at the time since almost everyone viewed the markets as a casino.

He defined investment as an operation that was carried out based on sound principles and had a high probability of success. The high probability of success resulted from the use of sound principles. This makes the principles an investor follows the central driver of profits. The stronger your principles, the higher your overall likelihood of long term profits.

Speculation, according to Graham, was the exact opposite of this. It was carried out using unsound principles and was implemented to earn unrealistic results. It's crucial to recognize that Graham did not include the names of any instruments when defining these terms. He merely characterized them.

In his own career, Graham used all kinds of instruments for investment purposes. He passed this habit onto his greatest student, Warren

Buffett. Buffett used all kinds of weird instruments when he started out working in Graham's investment firm. One of his more famous investments was exchanging shares of stock (that traded for $34) for cocoa beans certificates (valued at $36) and reselling the beans on the market for a $2 profit per share (Wathen, 2013).

This isn't an example of options trading, but it shows that the instrument used in investment isn't all that important as long as the principles are sound. If Buffett was simply betting on the value of cocoa bean futures to increase, he would have been speculating. Instead, he took advantage of an extraordinary situation where he purchased an asset worth $36 for $34.

Buffett would graduate to using far more complex instruments in his deals as his abilities grew. One of his more famous bets was negotiating a convertible preferred share deal with Goldman Sachs that netted him over a billion in profits for a very low investment.

There are other examples of investors using seemingly "risky" instruments to profit. Carl Icahn famously used call options to assume control of Herbalife during his feud with Bill Ackman (Belvedere, 2019). Icahn used options to leverage his investment and despite his bullish sentiments on the company, he clearly didn't want to risk a significant amount of capital on the bet. Options gave him the ability to profit if Herbalife went up and they also restricted his downside to an acceptable limit in case things went pear-shaped. Icahn seemingly entered the investment to spite Ackman, with whom he's had a long running feud, yet there's no doubt that his bullish sentiment on the company was founded on sound principles. At the end of the day, Icahn was right on the company (even though Ackman wasn't necessarily wrong).

OPTIONS AS INVESTMENT

The point of these stories is that you need to reassess the idea of a particular instrument being risky simply because of its structure.

Options can get extremely complicated, but this depends on the person using them. Someone who has traded options for over a decade will not find the advanced options strategies too complex.

Another investor who doesn't understand how calls or puts work is going to fail almost certainly at executing these strategies. The key is to match your abilities with appropriate strategies. It goes back to Buffett's warning about investors needing to stick to what they know, or their circle of competence, as he puts it.

If you're still on the sidelines, here's an example. When you read anything about the credit crisis that occurred between 2007 to 2009, you will come across the term Collateralized Debt Obligation or CDO. These were highly leveraged instruments that ultimately caused the meltdown. By all accounts, CDOs were the villain of the crisis. However, there were hedge funds that used CDOs to earn a profit (Baird, 2007). Like options, CDOs can represent many different assets. The key isn't to look at what the instrument is but what your investment thesis is. Anyone can misuse a tool and cause damage, this isn't the tool's fault.

MISUSING OPTIONS

The usual manner in which options are used is to implement them as a part of speculative strategies. Traders make short-term bets using options because they provide a lower cost of entry into the market. Instead of placing a directional bet, they use options to try to profit from the volatility spike that they foresee.

While there are trading strategies that use intelligent principles, there's no guarantee that traders use them in such a manner. A survey conducted by the brokerage firm FXCM revealed that 90% of their traders blow their account within a year (Russel, 2009). There are no statistics available publicly for stock traders, but anecdotal evidence suggests that the number may be even higher due to the larger number of people taking part in the stock market.

With such high failure rates, it stands to reason that options end up being viewed as risky. In fact, the stock market is viewed as being risky thanks to the prevalence of such statistics. As we highlighted in the previous section, it isn't the market or the instrument's fault. It's simply the phenomenon of the majority of people misusing market instruments.

If speculation is the opposite of investing, it stands to reason that an intelligent investor stands to gain by doing the exact opposite of what the average speculator does.

The most common manner in which most speculators trade options is to use them as tools to bet on price movements. If they think the price of a stock is about to rise, they buy call options. If they think it's about to fall, they buy puts. It's safe to say none of these directional trades work well consistently.

The thing for a smart investor to do is to take the opposite side of these trades. If there was a way to short these traders' activities, you'd stand to make a lot of money. In fact, many hedge funds do this already by designing ETFs that take advantage of common trader mistakes.

However, there is an easier way for the individual investor, and that's where options come in. Since most traders look to buy options, the thing for you as an intelligent investor to do is to write options to them. Most options trades fail because they end up expiring outside the money. If this is the case, it makes sense to align yourself with the best odds.

This is the core thesis behind writing covered calls: By writing options, you're placing yourself in a position of maximum success since the odds are in your favor right from the start.

HOW MANY OPTIONS EXPIRE WORTHLESS?

We must point out that there is a myth in this regard. The myth states that 85% of all options expire worthless. This is not true. In fact it's the result of a miscalculation by uninformed sources. This number is often quoted because the average researcher doesn't take into account the fact that a lot of options trades are closed out before expiry (Smith, 2019).

This doesn't mean you don't stand to gain an advantage by being a net seller of options. However, don't make the mistake of wildly exaggerating this advantage in your mind. You will read sources mentioning that you can align the odds in your favor much like a casino does and that you can expect win rates of above 85%. This is not true at all. Believing such false tales is to indulge in speculative behavior.

Another statistic that is often quoted is that only 10% of options contracts are ever exercised. This is used as evidence that only 10% of options finish ITM. However, that's a false leap of logic. Options can be sold prior to expiry if the buyer wishes to capture the increase in premium.

Often, options investors don't have the cash on hand to exercise the option. Recall our previous example about Amazon calls. You could have exercised the ITM call, bought stock and sold. It's far easier to simply sell the call itself and earn a profit. Close to 60% of options are closed out prior to expiry. This is done by both buyers and writers.

A writer might be looking to close out their position by covering their investment (by buying back the option) and capturing the decline in premium. Not every option writer allows their option to expire worthless. Sometimes, short-term volatility drives prices extremely low and they close it out in order to avoid a bounce up in prices prior to expiry.

Buyers close out their positions for reasons mentioned previously. The point is that the true number of options contracts that expire worthless is closer to 35% or so. This is still a significant number and places the odds in favor of option writers.

Our objective is to educate you with realistic numbers and statistics. While the strategy we're presenting requires you to sell options, we're not going to claim that this is foolproof or will make you a million dollars overnight. We're also going to resist making claims that cite the incorrect numbers we've highlighted. It's best to begin your options journey using sound investment principles, and this is what we'll be presenting to you throughout the remainder of the book.

Win Rates and Average Wins

Most speculators don't fully understand the role that win rates and average win amounts play in determining the profitability of a trading system. The average person chases a 100% win rate since this is how all of us have been conditioned since our childhood.

In our school days we were told to get as many answers right on our exams so that we could pass to the next level. We carry this behavior over to our workplace and live our lives chasing the right answers. In the markets this principle doesn't quite hold up, however. Having the right answers in the market is no guarantee of making money.

As an example, there are many traders who can correctly predict the short-term direction of the market. They still lose money. Why is this? It's because the markets are chaotic. They can go up, but before they do, they're perfectly capable of hitting your stop loss by declining and then rising.

The true way to make money in the markets is to ensure that you lose very little when you do lose and win a lot when you win. If you've ever traded before, you'll have heard the adage "cut your losses and let your winners run." This applies to pretty much any endeavor in the market. You need to remain invested for the right reasons, irrespective of what the price does. When the reasons change, you need to exit your position even if it's continuing to rise. Traders are more concerned with the price, and this is why they exit the trade if it goes against them.

On the other hand, investors aren't concerned (or shouldn't be) when the price moves up or down in the short term. Their thesis is the most important thing, so entry and exit depends on that entirely.

When it comes to writing options, the odds of being right and the option expiring outside the money are high. This means you'll win more often than not. However, the money that you'll make on these winners will be less, on average, than what an option buyer will make.

An option writer's challenge is to stick to their rules and not get carried away by their regular stream of wins. This is easier said than done. It's great to make money. It's easy to start thinking of yourself as the best investor ever when this happens. The key is to keep executing your strategy over and over.

Some investors sabotage themselves by demanding excitement. When everything is said and done, the covered call is a pretty boring strategy. It's not exciting and the money you receive will start becoming monotonous, even if such a state of affairs seems unrealistic to you right now.

As you read the rest of this book, keep these points in mind. You might get carried away at the thought of winning most of your positions, but recognize that the win amounts will be low. However, by repeatedly executing your strategy, you'll ensure that you have a safe and steady return.

FREEMAN COVERED CALL RULE #5

THE BEAUTY OF THE COVERED CALL IS NOT THAT
YOU WIN BIG. IT'S THAT YOU
WIN SMALL, AND OFTEN. MAKING IT A RELIABLE
AND REPEATABLE INCOME SOURCE

4

AN OVERVIEW OF COVERED CALLS

Now that you have a good foundation on options basics, it's time to explore the covered call strategy in more depth. The covered call is an entry-level strategy within options trading or investing. It's a safe strategy that limits your downside risk thanks to the way in which it's structured.

As described in the previous chapter, the covered call has a higher success rate because of the large number of options that expire worthless. Like many options trades, the strategy has two legs to it. Unlike regular stock investments, most options strategies will require you to open two separate positions. This sounds complicated, but it's quite straightforward when it comes to the covered call.

The reason is that one of your trade legs will already be open, so there's nothing additional you need to do. The two legs of the covered call strategy are:

1. A long stock leg
2. A short call option leg

LEGS OF THE TRADE

The long stock leg in the covered call is the regular investment you hold in your account. For example, if you hold Disney (DIS) stock, then you'll receive capital gains and dividends over time. While dividends do provide cash flow, they yield around two to three percent at best. Covered calls can generate a far higher rate of cash flow, as you'll shortly see.

We must mention that the long stock leg is implemented using your usual investment principles. You don't need to think of the covered call when buying the stock. The main point of the covered call is to monetize your existing investments for cash flow. Think of it as owning a car and using that car to make some extra cash every month. You wouldn't buy the car for the sole purpose of earning a few extra bucks.

Most investors hold their long stock legs in an individual retirement account (IRA). We advise against writing covered calls on investments held in a retirement account. This strategy is relatively straightforward, but there is a chance of you having to sell your long stock leg. If you do this from an IRA and withdraw the money, you'll end up paying a 10% penalty plus taxes. Note, that your stock being called away is not a taxable event in itself. However as the point of an IRA is to maximize your after-tax profits, using it to generate cash flow is not advisable.

For this reason, use a normal stock holding account with your broker when implementing the covered call. Something else to keep in mind is that you must own at least 100 shares of stock if you wish to use a covered call strategy. This is because each option contract covers 100 shares and you'll need this amount in stock holding to be able to execute a covered call. This is why you can execute covered calls with a Level 1 options trading account.

The second leg of the trade is a short or written call. We previously mentioned that writing a call is perhaps the riskiest thing a market participant can do. We must clarify that statement. Writing a *naked* call is the riskiest thing to do. Naked in this context doesn't refer to your clothes but to the nature of the call.

A naked call is something that isn't backed by equity or cash. Let's say you write a call on Amazon with a strike price of $4,000. You don't have any equity in your account (in the form of Amazon stock) or cash to cover the cost of assignment should the underlying rise enough to move the call into the money.

Remember that if you're assigned a call, you need to sell stock to the option buyer. If AMZN is selling at $4,500 when you're assigned the option, you'll need to buy it for this price and sell it to the option buyer for $4,000 (the strike price) for an instant loss of $500 per share. Every contract covers 100 shares, so that's a loss of $50,000.

This isn't even the worst-case scenario. The price of Amazon can theoretically rise till infinity. If it rose to $6,000 or more you'd probably bankrupt yourself. This is why selling a naked call is a risky thing. Most brokers will not allow you to do this even if you have a Level 4 or 5 options trading account.

However, they will allow you to do this with a Level 1 account if you cover your risk. How is this done?

COVERING YOUR CALL

As long as you own the underlying stock on which you're writing the call, your position is covered, hence the name covered call. In this scenario, if the option is assigned to you, you'll be able to deliver the stock to the buyer since you already own it. Your broker will automatically sell your stock holding to the buyer at the option's strike price.

This means you have zero risk of not being able to come up with the money to cover assignments. Your downside risk is always defined, and you won't even come close to losing too much money. The only scenario in which you'll lose money is when you buy the stock and then are immediately assigned the option. In this case your long stock leg won't have enough time to appreciate and you'll be stuck with a loss. However, this is an infrequent scenario and not something you'll likely ever encounter, even in a multi-year span of writing options.

IMPLEMENTING THE COVERED CALL

Here are the steps you need to take to implement the covered call:

1. Buy the stock (at least 100 shares to cover one options contract. If you plan on writing more contracts, you'll need to buy shares in multiples of 100)
2. Write calls.
3. Monitor your trade.

That's all there is to it. The only thing you need to take into account is the strike price of the calls.

For a quick video of how to write covered calls in your brokerage account, we have one on our YouTube channel, which you can find at

https://freemanpublications.com/youtube

Since you're writing calls, you're expressing an opinion that the price of the underlying stock won't rise beyond a certain point for as long as the trade is active.

Some investors get confused at this point. Buying the stock means you're bullish about it, so why would you sell calls against it? This is where the investment horizon of your strategy comes into play. Remember that the long stock leg is bought with the intention of holding onto it for a long time.

You might be bullish over the long term, but if you think the stock isn't going to do much over the short term, say the next month or so, then you can use covered calls to generate cash flow for yourself. Do this often enough and you'll manage to generate enough cash to significantly reduce the cost basis of your investment.

Cash comes in from writing the call. Recall that when you write a call, you receive the premium that the buyer pays. You'll get to keep this premium no matter what happens. If the option expires outside the money, you don't need to pay anything. If you're assigned the stock, your broker will sell the long stock leg at the strike price to the buyer of the option.

Choosing the strike price for your call is critical. You want to pick a price that is far enough away so as to reasonably expire OTM, but you also want it to be close enough to the underlying price so that the option premium is high.

Since you'll be writing OTM calls, they will have no intrinsic value. So the entire value of the option comes from the time value attached to them. Time value decays as the option you've written enters the last 30 days of expiry, therefore you want to choose options that expire beyond this term. Ideally, volatility will also be decreasing when you write the option, but this is something we'll address later.

A SAMPLE COVERED CALL TRADE

Let's look at an example of a covered call trade on Disney to see how it can make you money. For the purposes of this example, we'll assume that you own 100 shares of Disney stock that you bought for $80 per share. The current market value is $128 per share. This means your original investment was $8,000. This purchase was made with the intention of holding onto Disney for the long term since you like the company's prospects.

Since you're sitting on a decent amount of gains, you'd now like to generate some cash flow from this position. The covered call should ideally be implemented when you've already captured unrealized gains from your stock position. This way, even if you do get assigned the stock, you'll make money since you bought it at a lower price.

You take a look at Disney's chart and determine that $140 seems to be a level that it won't breach over the next month or so. We'll get into methods to reasonably determine this later in the book. For now our focus is on writing calls at the $140 level. We take a look at Disney's option chain and see that the 140 call, which will expire in 30 days, is selling for a premium of $0.59.

You'll need to multiply the price as stated by 100 to get the full contract's price since it's stated on a per share basis. This means if you write the 140 OTM call you'll receive $59 ($0.59*100) as cash, which will be deposited into your brokerage account immediately after you execute the trade. Now that both of your trade legs have been set up, here are the three scenarios that could play out.

Scenario One

The first scenario is if the option expires outside the money. This is your best-case scenario since you get to hold onto both the long stock leg, and also get to realize the full premium. Since the stock is OTM, it will expire worthless. As time progresses, you will see its value decreasing. Here is what the numbers look like in this scenario:

Long stock purchase price = $80
Long stock leg investment cost = $8,000 (80*100)
Premium received upon writing 140 call = $59
Return on investment = (59/8,000) = 0.73%
Annualized return before compounding = return on investment*12 = 8.85%
New cost basis of investment = (8,000 – 59) = $7,941
New effective purchase price of your stock = (7,941/100) = $79.41

We've used an annualized return, because this trade plays out over a period of just 30 days. Therefore it is completely possible to repeat the same trade 12 times over the course of a year.

This 8.85% annualized return is far higher than a dividend yield that you will realize by investing in most stocks. Even REITs don't pay such high yields. Besides, the annualized return doesn't take compounding into consideration.

You can reinvest your proceeds from the covered call to buy either more stock or invest it into something else that can further grow your portfolio.

There is another bonus to covered calls here, notice that your effective investment purchase price reduces. You've received cash and this increases the profit you've realized from the trade. Over time, you can reduce your cost basis significantly by writing calls. Assuming you earn this same amount of money for a year, you'll have made $708 as cash flow. This translates to a reduction of $7.08 per share in terms of the effective purchase price. So not only have you profited from selling calls, you've also increased your unrealized capital gains by lowering the cost basis of your stock position.

FREEMAN COVERED CALL RULE #6

COVERED CALLS ARE NOT JUST A GREAT INCOME
TOOL. THEY ALSO LOWER YOUR
COST BASIS ON YOUR LONG STOCK HOLDINGS

Scenario Two

The second scenario is if the option finishes in the money. If you happen to be wrong about the movement of Disney stock and if it exceeds $140 before expiry, you'll be assigned the option. What happens next? Your broker will sell the stock you hold at the call's strike price. You will get to keep the option premium that you earned when you wrote the call. Here's what the numbers look like:

Cost of stock investment = $8,000
Purchase price = $80
Sale price = $140
Premium received from writing calls = $59
Total profit = (140 - 80)*100 + 59 = $6,059
Rate of return = 75%

The only difference between this scenario and the previous one is that you will lose your long stock position. This results in a much higher realized gain since you'll have to sell your stock holding. However, if the stock is rising you'd ideally like to participate in its rise. What if Disney rose to $170 over the next year? You won't be able to take full advantage of this rise.

Having said that, since you bought the stock for $80, you won't lose money even if you're assigned the option. In theory you could even buy the stock at the market currently for $128 and realize a profit of $12 per share if the option finishes ITM.

However, it's inadvisable to do this. What if the option finishes OTM? In that case you'll have to hold onto the stock and wait for it to pass the price for which you bought it. If it declines for years on end, then your capital losses will outweigh whatever cash flow you earn. This is why we recommend initiating covered calls on positions that already have enough of a profit cushion built into them.

Scenario Three

The third scenario that can occur is if the underlying finishes ATM on expiry. In this case you'll be assigned the option and the numbers are exactly the same as in the previous scenario. The price to which it rises is of no consequence to you since your selling price is fixed by the strike price of the call.

In determining these numbers we haven't taken commissions into account. Your broker may also charge an assignment and exercise fee and this is why many options trades look to avoid it. This is why most traders close their positions before expiry if they're in a profit. Assignment fees aren't significant, but over time they will eat into your gains. Your best scenario is for the option to finish OTM. That way you can continue to hold onto your long stock leg and keep writing calls to earn cash on that investment.

WRITING COVERED CALLS VERSUS WRITING PUTS

Once you start running the numbers on different options strategies, you soon find out that writing a covered call has the same risk-reward profile as writing a put does. Which is why there is much discussion in options trading circles about whether it is better to write a put in some cases, since it's a single leg trade as opposed to the covered call, which has two legs.

There's just one problem with this line of thought. Brokers will not allow beginner options traders to write naked puts. Even if you did have the cash required to cover the risk of a naked put, take a moment to think about what each strategy implies.

Writing a covered call implies you're betting on the stock to not rise beyond a certain point. Writing a naked put implies you're bullish on a stock above a certain point. A lot of traders look at the risk to reward profiles of these strategies using the same strike prices. However, it makes no sense to look at it this way. If a stock is trading at $100, you'll write an OTM call above this price and an OTM put below it. Writing an option that is in the money is an extremely risky strategy since you don't know when it'll be assigned to you.

The traders who do things this way bet on the chance that their options won't get assigned or that the underlying will quickly move out of the money and they'll be off the hook. This way, they capture the intrinsic value in the premium for as long as the option is ITM. Couple this with time decay and you have a recipe for huge profits.

However, this is not a repeatable strategy in any way. If the stock doesn't move away from the money, you will almost certainly be assigned the option and lose money on the trade.

The bottom line is that you need to stay away from writing puts. Any arguments that push their efficacy over writing covered calls ignores the fact that you're an investor, not a speculator looking to make a quick buck.

PROFIT AND LOSS NUMBERS FOR THE COVERED CALL

Let's quickly run through the maximum profit and loss numbers for the covered call strategy.

Maximum Profit

The maximum profit you'll receive is calculated as follows:

Maximum profit = (Strike price - stock purchase price) + premium received

This scenario occurs if you're assigned the stock. Don't get confused and think this is all you can earn. One of the things to remember about the covered call is that the long stock position makes it tough to quantify exact maximum profit and loss numbers. For example, the option could finish OTM and earn the premium in full.

This means you'll hold onto the long stock position, which can theoretically rise for as long as possible. It could also decline to a value of zero. This makes calculating an exact number tough. To make the maximum profit quantifiable, we've assumed that you'll be assigned the option. However, this isn't the best-case scenario as we've explained previously.

. . .

Maximum Loss

Like with the maximum profit number, we've had to make some assumptions to quantify it. In order to do so we've assumed the worst-case scenario for everything. We've assumed that the option will finish OTM but the long stock position will decline all the way to zero. The probability of this happening is low, but it is a valid scenario nonetheless.

However, we must mention that this trade has the same risk profile as holding the long stock. Writing the covered call doesn't add any additional risk. This means the maximum loss can be calculated as:

Maximum loss = Stock purchase amount - premium received

The break-even point of your trade will be the purchase price minus the premium received. The premium you'll receive will lower your cost basis as explained. We'd like to reiterate that the maximum profit and loss scenarios here do not necessarily reflect the best and worst-case scenarios. The presence of the long stock leg complicates calculations.

You should always look to have your call finish OTM and hang onto your long stock leg. The best-case scenario is for you to partake in the capital gains from your investment and keep earning steady cash flow on it using covered calls.

Something else to keep in mind is that since you'll be owning the stock, all dividends that will be paid during this time will accrue to you. These dividends will also increase your profit and reduce your loss. If you happen to have been an owner of the stock as of the ex-dividend date, losing the stock position will not affect receipt of the dividends. You'll still receive them, and this will reduce your cost basis even further.

5

THE TWO BEST REASONS TO WRITE COVERED CALLS

There are many advantages to writing covered calls, but two stand out above everything else. There are some investors who believe covered calls are risky and loath to place their long stock position at risk of being called away. This is understandable. However, if you're looking to generate income from your investments, simply sitting on your position is also not a smart move.

Recall the previous comparison we made to real estate investment, where investors regularly generate cash flow from their properties. You won't lose cash due to sitting on your investment, but you will incur opportunity costs. The best way to illustrate this is with an example.

From the previous chapter, we saw that writing covered calls on Disney stock produced an annual return of around eight percent. This is a pretty significant return. Coupled with the stock market's average performance of 10% per year, this will yield a significant gain for you over time. The best part is that this eight percent return can be reinvested into other opportunities.

Let's say you have $5,000 invested in Disney and are receiving eight percent in cash every year. Let's assume that Disney performs at the market average and returns a steady 10% per year for 20 years. This means you'll have $5,500 at the end of the first year. If you were to simply hang onto this principal without looking to generate cash against it, you'd do very well over a 20-year span. After the end of the 20-year period, you would end up with $30,580.

Now, what happens if you generate eight percent per year from covered call writing and reinvest it back into the stock? By doing this, not only are you compounding your original principal, you're also compounding the eight percent you're generating as cash. At the end of the 20-year mark, you'll have $116,072 in your account. That's a 279% increase in capital. This scenario assumes you won't be making any contributions to the account over the 20-year period.

So what happens if you were to contribute an additional sum of $1,000 every month for a $12,000 annual contribution? In the first scenario, where you hang onto your investment solely for capital gains, you'll have $644,488 in your account, which is a handsome sum.

However, in the covered call case, you'll have $1,597,034 in your account. You'll more than double your money in the same time frame by following this strategy.

Aside from the numbers highlighting the stark differences, we must also consider where covered calls really shine using the phenomenon of asymmetric returns.

ASYMMETRIC RETURNS AND SYNTHETIC DIVIDENDS

Let's tackle asymmetric returns first. In the previous example, we outlined that the stock market returns around 10% per year. Over the long term this is the case, however, it doesn't return a flat 10% per year on autopilot. The market moves up and down and even loses you money in some years. Many investors don't have the stomach to hang onto their investments during the tough times and end up selling precisely when they should be buying.

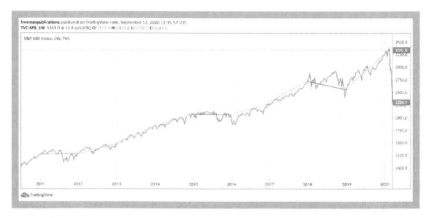

Figure 2: The annual returns of the S&P 500 index between 2011 and 2019. In the past nine years, there were six bullish years, one flat year and two years (2015 and 2018) where the index declined

Figure 2 illustrates the annual returns of the S&P 500, over the past nine years. While the overall trend has been upwards, with an average gain of 11.7% per year over this 9 year period. There are many periods where the market has either remained flat or dipped and wiped out its previous gains. We'd also like to remind you that this run you're seeing in Figure 2 happens to represent the longest bull market run that American markets have ever witnessed.

Even in such record-breaking markets, you can see that the market has had years where it has been unfriendly towards investors. The fact is that investors need all the help they can get when it comes to managing their emotions. These kinds of gyrations where the market gains 20% one year and then declines by 50% the next tend to make investors very nervous.

The average investor follows the financial news media quite closely and is likely to buy into the hype or hysteria, depending on what the media is selling at that moment. If you're looking at holding on for the long term and rely on just capital gains, you'll need to possess high levels of emotional strength.

Assuming you have this, there is another problem. Inflation continually eats away at your gains. With the current money printing policies in place, it's a given that inflation will increase at some point down the road. If you're like the average investor, you're looking at holding onto your position for at least a decade. This means you're seeing your gains being eaten into even when they rise and especially when they fall.

What would make your life easier? Inflation and taxes aren't going to go away anytime soon, so you might as well not hope for that scenario.

Earning a dividend is an attractive proposition. If you could earn cash flow while you held onto your investments, that would be great. The issue with dividends is that they come directly from the bottom-line profits of the companies that pay them.

We explained this previously in the book. A company's stock price rises in line with its earnings over the long term. Any payment from these profits potentially detracts from capital gains increases. Besides, companies that pay dividends have usually left their high growth days behind them. You're placing your money in these companies to preserve capital and increase cash flow as a best-case scenario.

Capital gains are present, but these stable dividend payers aren't the kinds of companies that will make you wealthy. For example, companies such as Amazon don't pay dividends and probably never will thanks to the enormous cash flow requirements they have. Investing in dividends for the cash flow gives you a yield of two to three percent at best.

There are companies that pay higher yields, of course, but these are a bit unsafe. There isn't any company out there paying 20% of its earnings and yielding eight percent. Such a combination is preposterous and will probably not last for very long. Either the company will go bust or the market will adjust the price for which the shares sell.

REIT dividends tend to pay high yields, but once again you'll not be earning much in the way of capital gains. These companies grow at the average rate at which their real estate appreciates and this isn't all that much. In essence, they behave like companies that are present in the Dividend Aristocrats Index.

The solution to this is to generate a *synthetic dividend*. Synthetic here refers to an external source that behaves as an asset that produces cash flow. The asset in this case is the covered call that you will write. If you're earning eight percent yields per year on your investment, then you won't mind hanging onto your investment through tough times will you?

It's a bit like buying a property and then seeing its price drop. If your tenants are paying you enough to realize an eight percent yield, you're probably not going to sell the place anytime soon. Consistent cash flow puts your mind at ease and helps you remain calm. You'll be able to ignore the constant shouting in the media. This is where the entire concept of earning "rental income" on your stocks comes from.

The great thing about covered calls is that they work very well over the course of a year. You'll initiate them in 30-45 day intervals, which removes the need for you to predict what the stock price will look like in a year. All you need to do is look at the reasonable level to which prices might rise over a month, and that's it.

For the most part, stocks act the same as the market average. They don't just trend slowly upwards throughout the year. They experience perhaps one of two good trending moves in a year, but the rest of time, move sideways. We've illustrated this in Figure 3 below.

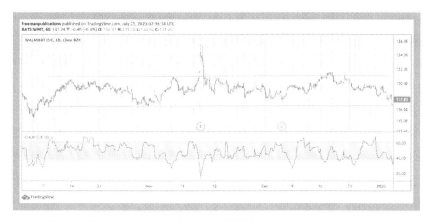

Figure 3: The hourly chart for Wal-Mart (WMT) between October 7th 2019 and January 3rd 2020.

Except for a couple of quickly corrected after-hours moves, Wal-Mart stock traded between $116 and $121 for 90 days straight. This would have been a perfect opportunity for Wal-Mart stockholders to earn additional income with some covered calls. Note the numbers on the Choppiness index on the bottom of the image; we'll be discussing how important those are later.

This chart indicates that for the vast majority of the year, your investment isn't making you money. It's just sitting there doing nothing. Forcing it to earn you a synthetic dividend by writing covered calls will boost your investment returns immensely, as you've already seen. These sideways periods are perfect for you to earn some additional cash.

In fact, in such markets, you can get away with writing calls that are closer to the underlying price. The sideways movement ensures that the probability of prices rising is remote. You'll earn greater premiums on the calls you write as a result.

REDUCING COST BASIS

The second advantage of generating synthetic dividends is the reduction they provide to your cost basis. A reduction in cost basis also helps you hang onto your investment for longer since you can withstand more significant capital losses.

From the previous example of Disney, we can see that the covered call premiums amount to around eight percent per year. This means your cost basis is reduced by this amount every year. If you bought Disney for $80, within three years your effective purchase price will be $58. If the stock were to decline to $70 during this period, it wouldn't cause you any problems since your effective purchase price is so much lower than that.

This effect is present in regular dividends as well, especially in REITs. However, the way the IRS handles REIT taxation means you won't get as many benefits from it as you would with covered call options. A portion of REIT dividends are considered return of capital and this reduces your cost basis.

However, the IRS taxes your capital gains from that reduced cost basis when you sell. This means you'll pay capital gains taxes on it no matter what. If you receive enough dividends, then your tax bill will be high despite paying them at the reduced long-term capital gains tax rate.

This isn't the case with option writing. Your premiums will be treated as income and you'll pay the marginal tax rate. However, you'll not be charged capital gains taxes from the effective cost basis. This means should you choose to sell your stock for the price of $70, the IRS views this as a capital loss. However, in reality, you've earned a gain of $12.

You can use this capital loss to offset other gains and reduce your tax bill. While this isn't a direct effect of covered call writing, it is an added bonus. A reducing cost basis means your capital gains are increasing by the premium earned every time you write covered calls.

This is a great thing to have going for you. Combine this with the compounding effect, and your investment value will skyrocket. Admittedly, both of these benefits are connected to one another, so it isn't as if you'll realize gains from them separately. However, the underlying cash flow that you'll generate is what powers these two benefits.

Once you begin to prioritize generating cash flow from your investments, you'll manage to increase the rate at which your money compounds. You'll also be able to hold onto your positions despite the hysteria that surrounds the markets.

6

DEBUNKING 4 COMMON MYTHS

There are a few myths floating around about covered calls. Some of these arise from legitimate concerns around covered calls, while some are just flat-out nonsensical. In this chapter we're going to clarify these situations and help you better understand how you can go about executing covered calls.

MYTH ONE - COVERED CALLS CAN ONLY BE WRITTEN AGAINST STOCKS

This is a pretty big myth and causes a lot of damage to investors. It results from a lack of knowledge of how options work and how they differ from stocks. As a stock investor you've probably realized that you cannot buy an index. Indices are not tradable instruments. They're simply a snapshot of a certain group of securities.

If you're like most intelligent investors, you probably follow an indexing strategy to some extent with adequate diversification. This is an indirect way of taking advantage of stock indices. They're designed to increase in value over the long term thanks to keeping up with inflation and screening in the best companies automatically.

It isn't guaranteed that the index funds and ETFs that track them will be able to capture all of their gains. Most of them lag to a certain extent thanks to incurring trading costs and having to constantly maintain their portfolio weights. Stocks therefore, don't offer you a direct method of profiting from index movements, even though index funds are a very good option.

This is not the case when it comes to options contracts. You can buy calls and puts on indices directly. This allows you to benefit from the underlying moves. There are options available on the S&P 500, the Dow Jones Industrial Index and so on. As a result you can run the covered call strategy on index options.

It might seem a bit confusing at first. The covered call strategy assumes that you will hold a long position in the underlying. However, you can't buy an index. Different brokers handle this differently. Some of them are fine, with you holding a collection of stocks that are on the index. Some brokers insist on the investor holding a representative piece of the index in their portfolios. You'll need to check with your broker about this.

Other details to watch out for when executing covered calls (or any options strategy against index options) is that they're European or they're cash-settled. Let's tackle the European bit first.

European options, if you recall from earlier in the book, can only be exercised on the day of expiry. They cannot be exercised at any other times. Certain exceptions exist, but these are low in number. For the most part, if you're in a long strategy (buying an option) you'll have a rough time of it. However, for the writer of an option, European options are great. The probability of an asset finishing at exactly the strike price or above it for one single day is lower as opposed to it moving into the money over a longer period of time.

This means European option premiums are lower since the writer has the upper hand in the deal. However, the writer has a greater probability of gaining the premium without having to worry about assignment. This makes the covered call strategy on index options a very reliable one. Your cash yield will be low, but if safe cash flow is your priority, then owning a basket of the major index stocks and writing index options against it could be worth your while.

Cash settlement is the other feature of index options you need to be aware of. Since there is no underlying instrument, if you happen to be assigned the option, your broker will settle the trade in terms of the cash difference an exercise would have cost you.

For example, if option exercise would have resulted in you buying the underlying for $100 and selling it for $90 per share, your loss would have been $10 per share. Your broker will simply debit this amount instead of you having to physically close your positions. Thus, you'll manage to hang onto your basket of index-related stocks even if you happen to be assigned the option.

Index options have different volatility characteristics and they tend to adhere to the standards of the VIX. However, some of the smaller indices might have their own whims. You should take the time to study these indices before deciding to write calls against them.

Another option you can use to take advantage of market indices is to write options against index funds and ETFs that track them. All of the major index funds have options on them and this can be a great way for you to benefit. Keep in mind that you'll be indirectly betting on the movement of the index. In essence, you'll be using a derivative to bet on the movement of a derivative of the index.

However, these options are American in nature and their premiums are higher. As a result you stand to earn more income than with regular index options.

MYTH TWO: COVERED CALLS CANNOT BE WRITTEN IN AN IRA

We've mentioned the scenario where you could write covered calls in an IRA. There is a belief that this isn't possible for some reason thanks to the tax-advantaged nature of an IRA. This is not the case at all. While an IRA does have contribution limits, there are no limits on the kind of assets you can hold within them.

The Roth IRA does not allow you to hold real estate properties within it, but there are no restrictions on holding financial market instruments. If you end up making a ton of money writing calls against your IRA holdings, then these will be tax-free until you withdraw them. This gives you greater scope to compound your holdings.

That's the good news anyway. The bad news is that if your strategy doesn't work or if you don't choose the right strike prices to write your call at, you stand to lose your long position. If you sell the holdings in an IRA, you can leave it as cash in the account, but you can't withdraw it. This will attract a penalty of 10% plus any taxes you owe on the gains.

There are investors who write covered calls in their IRAs and 401(k)s. The latter especially provides immense benefits thanks to employers matching your contributions. This free cash can cause some people to become reckless and start employing strategies that promise to make them a lot of money in a short period.

We don't mean to say that you should never write covered calls in a retirement account or that it's an unsuccessful strategy. It's just that the point of a retirement account is to stash your cash away passively into an investment and not worry about losing it. Employing an active strategy in such an account doesn't always make sense.

Covered calls are a step above passive investing strategies because you need to return to them every month and also monitor your investment every day to make sure you're not in danger of assignment. This can get stressful if you have a particularly large long investment position.

The only situation in which you should write covered calls in a retirement account is when you have enough of a long position that you can dedicate a very small portion of it to writing covered calls. For example, if you hold 500 shares of a stock, then you can dedicate 100 shares and write a single contract.

The tax-free nature of your investments coupled with the increased compounding in a retirement account means you can rely on it to beat inflation pretty easily. This isn't the case in a regular investment account, which is why writing covered calls in investment accounts makes sense.

If you still wish to write covered calls in a retirement account, then make sure you have a backup plan to invest the cash you'll have left over if you're forced to sell your long position. Also make sure you've amassed enough of an unrealized capital gain before choosing to write covered calls.

Something to note is that you can write options only on self-directed IRA accounts. If your account is being managed by another investment firm, you can't implement the covered call strategy. But you can convert your managed IRA to a self-directed one pretty easily. You can notify the firm in charge of your IRA and request to convert it. You'll have to notify your broker as well if this isn't done automatically by the management firm. Once this is done, you're free to write options in the account.

A potentially lucrative investment option is to combine dividend investing with covered call writing. Your money will compound at the highest rate possible since you won't be charged any taxes. Take care to write calls at sensible levels, though. Don't get carried away by the high premiums of options that are close to the money. You'll only find yourself having to reallocate cash and then having to wait as your unrealized capital gains build up.

It's far better to focus on holding onto the long stock position since this will ensure you'll be writing calls at sensible levels and will not be chasing high yields on your investment just for the sake of them.

MYTH THREE: YOU WILL NOT RECEIVE DIVIDENDS ON STOCKS YOU WRITE CALLS AGAINST

The origin of this myth is a bit of a head-scratcher, but it exists nonetheless. Some investors believe that writing calls is akin to taking a short position, and therefore you will not receive dividends. It's made worse by the fact that many brokers allow you to enter a covered call trade via a buy-write order.

A buy-write order is one where you simultaneously enter a long stock position and write a call against that stock position. Needless to say, this is a speculative position to take since you don't have enough capital gains built up or indeed any built into your long stock position.

The combination of these two orders makes it seem as if they're joined at the hip. Investors feel that one cancels the other and therefore, you won't be entitled to receive dividends. As far as the company whose stock you hold is concerned, they don't particularly care that you've written a call against your position.

You're still a shareholder on their records and are entitled to receive all the benefits that are due to such a position. Take care to note the ex-dividend date. As long as the option's expiration date is after this, you'll receive a dividend even if you're assigned the option.

A bigger problem is the psychological discomfort some investors feel when they write calls against the stocks they own. The feeling is that they've been rooting for the stock to rise and now are somehow wanting it to remain in place. This feels like a betrayal of sorts for them.

For starters, investing in anything for emotional reasons is not intelligent investing. Suppose you find yourself becoming emotionally attached to your investments to the point where you start thinking of them fondly or use your account balance to make yourself feel better. In that case, you need to take a step back and review why you invested your money in the first place.

You're not rooting for anything. It's just a means of making money, and you should not be getting emotional about it. Focus your energies on doing the intelligent thing and take care of the basics of the strategy. This will ensure that you do the right thing and won't get emotionally carried away.

Some traders try to time writing covered calls with dividend announcement dates. During such times the stock price of the company in question rises in anticipation of the dividend. This ensures a small capital gain. Add to this the dividend as well as the covered call premium and you have the recipe of a strategy that can make you a lot of money on an annualized basis.

Should you follow such a strategy? This isn't an investment strategy and is based entirely on the public perception of a stock. The dividend announcement can go the other way as well. If the company announces a dividend cut, then the price will crash, leaving you with a capital loss. The call premium and the reduced dividend won't make up for it.

Such strategies have a whiff of "get rich quick" about them. This doesn't mean the strategy won't work. It's just that the amount of time you'll spend implementing and monitoring it is better spent elsewhere. Spend an additional hour or so at your regular job and earn overtime or spend that time creating another source of income.

MYTH FOUR: COVERED CALL WRITING WORKS BEST BEFORE SPECIAL EVENTS

This myth is closely connected to the previous one, and it comes from the way in which many options strategies are structured. As we mentioned earlier, options allow you to bet directly on the volatility prospects of a stock. You can short volatility or go long on it, depending on the conditions as you evaluate them.

Volatility is primarily created due to special announcements. These can be earnings announcements, certain company event-related press releases such as restructuring, dividend cuts, the result of a lawsuit, a merger, an acquisition etc. There are also macroeconomic announcements such as the release of interest rate announcements, the release of notes from the Federal Reserve Bank's monthly meetings, press conferences that announce new monetary policies and so on.

All of these events cause unpredictable price movements, and in many cases, create unpredictable volatility as well. Options allow you to profit no matter what happens. For example, a common volatility-based strategy is the straddle. In this trade, an options trader profits no matter which direction the stock's price moves.

It makes sense for a straddle trader to look at special events and time their trades accordingly. It doesn't quite make sense for a covered call trader because this is a directional strategy. Covered calls require prices to be under the strike price for the trader to earn a profit. This is not the case with non-directional strategies that don't depend on the direction of the price move.

By trying to time your covered call execution with a special announcement, you're explicitly expressing the view that you believe this announcement will not be great for the company's short-term prospects.

Of course, if the trade works out in your favor and if the announcement is bad for the company, then you'll get to keep the option premium and might even be able to buy more of the company's stock at a lower price. However, it's still speculation. You don't know what the effect of a news release will be. More often than not, the market has already accounted for the news impact in the stock price.

The stock markets are governed by strict insider trading rules and prevent institutions from gaining an unfair advantage. Everyone is privy to the same information, and the SEC does a very good job of enforcing these rules.

However, this doesn't mean informational advantages don't exist. Most institutions operate in the bond markets, which are much larger than the stock market. Unlike the stock markets, bond markets don't have insider trading rules. Everyone's an institutional player, and the SEC figures that everyone knows what they're doing. Bond prices often affect stock price movements, and many stock traders keep an eye on bond price movements.

Bonds are affected by a company's prospects just as much as stocks are. While it's tough to correlate stock and bond price movements exactly, a relationship does exist. Therefore, many institutional traders have orders locked and ready to go prior to the announcement. The average retail trader/investor is simply hoping that they're on the right side of the announcement.

Writing a covered call based on your prediction of an announcement with all of these factors in place is madness. Instead, it's far better to be conservative and to assume a defensive position by writing covered calls every month. This way, you can focus on generating steady cash flow for yourself without having to worry about what kind of price moves you'll have to account for.

We must stress that you still need to take news announcements into account. It's not as if you can simply ignore what's going on with your stock investment. Our point is you shouldn't try to time your strategy on the basis of special events. Instead, stick to your regular monthly schedule of writing covered calls and factor special events into your choice of strike prices.

This brings to a close our look at some of the myths that surround covered calls. It takes some time to understand why they're invalid, and we would suggest going back and revisiting these myths from time to time.

7

COVERED CALL "RISKS"

Although covered calls themselves do not cause additional risk to your stock position (hence the term "risk-free" in the title of this book), no investing strategy exists without risks.

In order to figure out whether writing covered calls suits you or not, you need to fully understand what you're getting into. There are three areas in particular that you should be aware of. All of these can be mitigated by adhering to a simple rule.

FREEMAN COVERED CALL RULE #8

IN A COVERED CALL, THE RISK IS IN THE UNDERLYING
STOCK OR INDEX, NOT IN THE OPTION

RISK ONE - STOCK PRICE APPRECIATION

This sounds like an odd thing to identify as a risk. After all, the covered call guarantees a profit if the stock price appreciates. The call is written at a higher level and if the option moves into the money, we'll end up selling the long stock leg for a higher price. So where's the risk in this?

The problem with the stock appreciating is that you'll incur a significant opportunity cost. Your reward is always capped at the level at which you'll write the call. This leaves you with the opportunity for a small profit, but you won't be able to participate in any further price appreciation.

Let's look at an example. Let's assume you initiated a covered call position on Disney when it was at $100 and wrote the call at $110. Let's say that at expiry, the price has moved all the way up to $190. In this scenario, your maximum profit is limited to the premium you earn by writing the call plus the difference between the strike price and the stock's purchase price. This equates to a little over $10 per share.

However, if you had simply bought the stock and left it at that, you would have earned a profit of $90 per share. You've given up $80 in profit per share in exchange for a smaller premium that you received in exchange for writing the call. It doesn't take a genius to figure out that this is not a very good trade. It's a bit like someone offering you the choice of $2 in profit or $80 in profit and you choose the former option.

There's no predicting how prices will behave in advance, so it's not a fully relevant comparison. However, over the long run, if you use covered calls to speculate, you will run into such scenarios. If you write calls at incorrect strike prices despite wanting to hold onto your stock for investment purposes, you'll still run this risk.

On the surface of it, this risk is best avoided if you choose the right strike prices. However, the real trick to avoiding this risk is to make a mental shift and to look at covered calls as a little boost to your gains instead of being a primary driver of them. The real driver of gains is the long stock leg of the trade.

This is what makes you the large capital gains which make people wealthy. You need to prioritize holding onto the stock at all costs. Of course, your initial investment decision needs to be based on how good of an investment the stock is, as we mentioned previously. If you're buying stocks to benefit from the short-term price rise and to write covered calls on them, there are easier strategies to make money.

In such cases, it's easier to simply buy calls on the stock instead of writing a covered call. Why would you implement a two legged trade when a simple one legged trade will do the same job? You'll also encounter lower commissions with a one legged trade. Buying just the stock to speculate in short-term price rises requires significant capital.

However, buying the calls doesn't require as much capital and you can leverage your position safely. If the price declines or if your long call doesn't move into the money, you can simply let it expire. The covered call is meant for investors who already hold long positions with a decent level of capital gains built up in them already.

This puts them in a win-win situation, no matter what happens. If the stock price rises from the date of initiating the trade but doesn't move the option ITM, they earn the premium. If the option moves ITM, then they make significant capital gains plus the premium. If it declines, they earn the premium and still have a cushion of unrealized gains.

Make this mindset shift, and you'll avoid incurring this cost. In case you're still not convinced, here's a chart that ought to convince you.

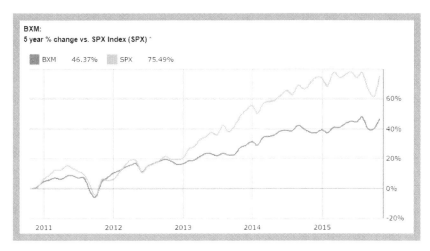

Figure 4: A graph showing a buy and hold strategy of the S&P 500 vs. a strategy which sold covered calls on the same index every month

Figure 4 shows the difference in gains between a strategy that simply bought the SPX versus a strategy that bought covered calls on the index every month and moved ITM. Notice how the covered call strategy makes money but its performance is far inferior to that of the SPX. Simply buying and holding would have been the better choice.

This does not mean that the covered call is a poor strategy. This scenario illustrates the importance of executing it for the right purposes. You should strive to write calls at levels that are unlikely to be hit, and write them at times when the market is flat rather than trending. You'll earn lower premiums, but this will be worth it because you'll supplement your capital gains and can reinvest your premiums into the stock purchase. That is what truly boosts gains and creates free leverage.

RISK TWO - STOCK PRICE DECLINES

This is the worst-case scenario for the covered call. What if the stock price declines and creates a capital loss. You'll then be faced with a decision to sell the stock or hold onto it in the hopes that its price rebounds. The option premium you'll receive will be scant relief in such situations.

There's no easy way to help you navigate the situation since so much depends on why you entered the long stock leg in the first place. If you're using the covered call for short-term profits, then the wise thing to do would be to follow sound trading principles and cut your losses.

You might be tempted to hold onto the stock, but this is not in line with what trading calls for. The worst thing a short-term trader can do is turn themselves into a long-term investor with a position.

If you bought the stock for long-term investment purposes and if the original investment thesis is still valid, then you ought to be delighted that the stock price has declined. You've earned income, and you get to buy the same asset for an even lower price. The trick is to evaluate the asset properly, of course.

Assuming you did that, this could very well be the best possible scenario for you. Your losses are still unrealized, and the lower stock prices will ensure that your cost basis will decrease even more. If the stock price keeps decreasing, you can write even more covered calls against your position and keep earning income on it.

So carefully evaluate your reason for entering the long stock leg. If your original investment reasoning is no longer valid, then it's best to take the loss and move on.

RISK THREE - MISMANAGEMENT

This is a small risk, but if you've become accustomed to monitoring just one leg in your investments, then the covered call adds a little complexity in that you now have two trade legs to monitor.

If you spot the market rising and moving your call closer to the money, and if you wish to hold onto your long stock leg for long-term investment purposes (as we recommend), it's best for you to cover your option position and take a small loss on the trade. You'll be compensated by the unrealized capital gains you'll earn from the appreciation of the stock leg.

Some investors prefer to remain completely passive with regard to their investments. If this applies to you, then initiating a covered call might not be the best choice. You will need to be aware of the price at which you wrote your call, as well as the stock's behavior. You might feel too much like a speculator and might suffer from additional anxiety thanks to market movements.

If you're not able to stop thinking about your short call's strike price, then you're better off avoiding this strategy. Exchanging a small profit for increased anxiety is not a recipe for success. The aim is to make money safely and sleep well at night.

8

THE RIGHT MARKET CONDITIONS FOR INITIATING COVERED CALLS

C overed calls might be a great way to generate a synthetic dividend, but to get the best out of them, you'll need to select the right market environment in which to initiate them.

Many covered call investors turn into traders and look to profit off the short-term moves of a stock. This is perfectly fine as long as your entry decisions are based on sound principles. If you've been an investor, then making short-term entry decisions might not be something you're familiar with. Short-term trading decisions require you to take technical analysis into account since these methods offer better insight into how the market behaves over the short term.

Many investors stay away from technical analysis because it looks like voodoo to them. We'll admit that certain technical analysis methods do nothing more than draw strange shapes on charts and pick and choose conditions that perfectly suit the chosen method. However, not all technical analysis methods are bogus.

In this chapter, we're going to share some of the best indicators and methods you can use to determine ideal conditions for the covered call. These methods apply irrespective of whether you're looking to hold onto your stock position for the long term or whether you're looking for a short-term profit by buying the stock and having it increase past the call's strike price.

TECHNICAL ANALYSIS IN 20 MINUTES

Before getting into the specific technical indicators you can use to determine ideal conditions for covered call writing, we'll have a brief overview of technical analysis. Newer investors often misunderstand technical analysis, and it's easy to be overwhelmed. Fortunately, there are only a few indicators you need to know to be profitable in terms of covered call writing. Before we cover these indicators, we'll briefly touch on what technical analysis truly aims to measure.

Fundamental analysis, which many long-term investors use, is primarily concerned with a business's economic prospects. On the other hand, technical analysis aims to measure the short-term drivers of a stock's price. Which is to say, it's aim is to try to spot the emotional direction of the market. This seems like a hopeless task at first glance. How well can you predict the emotions of someone you're close to and know very well? You could probably approximate their reactions by asking certain questions and reading their body language, but this wouldn't give you the whole picture.

So how can technical analysis help to predict the emotions of a million anonymous traders? The answer is quite simple. Technical analysis aims to identify the direction of the underlying order flow. This is the number of active buy or sell orders for a stock, which moves the price up or down.

Every indicator, at least the ones that work, captures this in one form or another. There are different types of indicators, but all of them fall into one of the following categories:

- Trend-based
- Oscillators
- Mathematical
- Geometric

Of all of these, the first two types are the ones that do the best job of capturing underlying order flow. All of them are derived from prior price behavior and present us with a picture of what is most probable. Something to note here is that there are no indicators that can predict the future. All of them are lagging by nature and not leading. The point of this discussion is to show you that even something that is largely speculative can have elements of logic to it.

We'll begin with trend-based indicators, which aim to capture the existing force with which price moves in a given direction. All of them capture the strength of a price move, whether it's up or down.

Many people misuse trend indicators because they rely on them to predict the direction in which prices might move. This is not what these indicators are for. In order to predict price direction, it's often best to look at the chart directly. Since we won't be concerning ourselves with predicting the possible direction of price, there's no reason to spend time understanding this.

Oscillators measure short-term momentum in price moves. They're usually bound between two extremes, typically 0 and 100. They also have zones on their charts which indicate levels where the stock is oversold and overbought. Typically, the oversold zones are at the bottom and the overbought ones are at the top. The idea is that if the stock lingers in the oversold zone for too long, it's due for a bounce and vice versa.

However, most oscillators don't work in a trending environment. When prices move strongly in a certain direction these indicators can print extreme values for a long time and this is also a trap that many traders fall into.

Mathematical indicators are our entry point into the voodoo territory of technical analysis. The most famous of these indicators are the Fibonacci projections. The Fibonacci series is a series of numbers where a number is the sum of the two that preceded it. For example 0,1,1,2,3,5,8 and so on is a Fibonacci sequence.

As it applies to technical analysis, Fibonacci levels are measured as a proportion of the pullback in a trend. Some of the most relevant Fibonacci levels are 100%, 61.8%, 50% and 33%. The idea is that once a price begins to pull back downwards from an uptrend, or upwards from a downtrend, prices always react at these levels. In the case of an uptrend, traders measure the length of the upswing and then mark the 33% level from the top of the push upwards.

They lay in wait at this level to watch for signs of prices being supported and being pushed back upwards. The same is done in the case of a downtrend. There is no earthly reason these levels ought to work. The markets don't care about random mathematical levels.

However, as with everything to do with emotions, the markets work in weird ways. Thanks to the Fibonacci levels' immense popularity, markets *do* react at these proportions of their up or downswings. This is because almost every trader out there believes in these levels and therefore, they become valid. Much like the phenomenon where if you hear something repeated to you over time, you begin believing it whether it's a fact or not. In this respect, Fibonacci levels work.

Lastly, we have geometric patterns, which people often think of when they hear the phrase "technical analysis." These are the most subjective of all technical analysis indicators.

You may have heard of some of these terms like *cup and handle, head and shoulders, double top* and *double bottom*. These are all just names for specific shapes you can draw onto a stock's price chart, and then use these shapes to determine which direction the stock is expected to go. That's the theory anyway.

Entire 1000 page books have been written just on geometric indicators. However, in practice, most geometric technical analysis "experts" are merely people looking to sell expensive courses or chatroom subscriptions, not those who use these geometric patterns to make money. You can think of it like the 19th Century gold rush, where the people who made the most money were the ones selling shovels, rather than people digging for gold.

A few geometric indicators are useful, such as understanding support and resistance lines and basic reversal/continuation patterns. However, beyond these, there isn't much use for geometric patterns in covered call writing.

Now we've had a high level look at technical analysis; we'll now be discussing a few technical indicators that will help you understand how to predict the short-term flow of markets.

Choppiness Index

The Choppiness Index is an indicator used to identify whether the price of an asset is trending in a direction or moving sideways. It aims to measure the degree to which a market is trending.

The Choppiness Index is an oscillator and is bound by values between a range of zero to 100. The closer the value is to 100, the higher the sideways movement of the stock or asset. Values that are close to zero indicate a trending market. The indicator doesn't give you any measurements with regard to the direction of the trend. A strong uptrend will print the same values as a strong downtrend.

The common threshold values that indicate extreme values are the Fibonacci retracements levels of 61.8 for the higher threshold and 38.2 for the lower threshold. Again, the Fibonacci levels are used here because many traders consider them to be valid. There's no order flow-based reasoning to this particular aspect of the indicator. Our recommendation is to study the stock for a while to determine extreme levels. Use the Fibonacci levels as a starting point and then refine it after a while. Rest assured that the exact demarcation of these extreme levels doesn't influence the indicator's effectiveness.

This is because the Choppiness Index derives itself from the order flow. Its values are calculated from the recent history of price moves. If prices are clustered together, this means they're moving in a tight range, and the index prints a high value. The farther apart they are, the lower the value is.

If the index line crosses the upper extreme from below, it is an indication that the market is most probably moving sideways. Typically this can be verified by simply looking at the chart. Again, the exact definition of this extreme level is not important. Every stock will have its own threshold, and you should spend some time studying the way it moves to figure out this location. If the line dives below the lower extreme, the market is likely to be a trending one. Once again, remember that the indicator doesn't provide directional guidance. It simply measures the trendiness or the degree of the sideways movement in the market. Figure 5 illustrates the Choppiness Index in Disney stock.

Figure 5: An example of a sideways market in Disney

As you can see in Disney's daily chart in Figure 5, when the Choppiness Index crossed the higher 61.8 threshold, it traded in a range (sideways movement) for 29 trading sessions or 42 days. This would have been a great time for Disney shareholders to earn extra income by selling covered calls to collect more premiums by selling strikes equal to recent highs.

In Figure 3, we highlighted the sideways movement in Wal-Mart stock, which is also an example of how the choppiness indicator can be used to determine the trending versus ranging state of the market. In these charts we've used the Fibonacci levels for ease of illustration.

So now, we've learned how the Choppiness Index is an oscillator that you can use to identify a sideways move. Let's look at an example of using a trend indicator to do the same.

Average Directional Index

The average directional index, or ADX, is one of those evergreen indicators we mentioned earlier. It's a pretty simple yet powerful indicator to use. The premise is simple. Anytime the indicator prints a value greater than 25, a trend is on. Anything below this value indicates a range or sideways movement in the stock price.

Trend traders use the ADX to determine the relative strength of a trend. They usually look for values greater than 50 to enter a trend. This makes the ADX a very useful indicator for you, just as the choppiness oscillator is. Lower values of the choppiness indicator print when a trend is present. When the ADX prints values higher than 25 or even 50, you can figure out how strong the trend is.

Figure 6 illustrates how the ADX is represented on a chart.

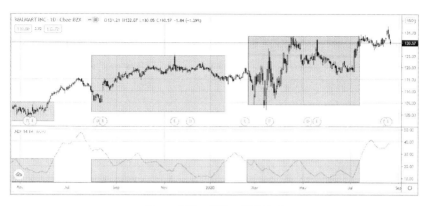

Figure 6: The ADX on Wal-Mart

Notice the areas colored by the boxes in Figure 6. This is where the indicator was below 25. Note the respective boxes on the price chart. The movement is invariably sideways. Like the choppiness indicator, the ADX doesn't provide any directional guidance. The only exception is the third box where we see initially choppy movement and then WMT makes a higher high despite the ADX remaining under 25.

This illustrates how no indicator is perfect and that you should take adequate precautions with all of your trades. In this scenario, notice how the range of each price bar widens. This shows that there is a possibility that volatility is increasing. As a result, strikes further OTM would have made more sense. In fact, that third box presents a great opportunity for covered call traders. Not only is the price movement largely sideways, volatility increases at first and then decreases. This would have meant that the OTM calls would have increased in value and then would have rapidly decreased.

Buyers would have paid you overpriced amounts for the calls, and you would have earned higher premiums despite being further OTM. However, as you can see from the price chart, volatility can be tricky to get right. This is why we urge you to use covered calls as a means of earning additional income on your long stock holdings. Volatility might change and you might find yourself choosing incorrect strike prices.

Between the choppiness index and ADX, you have all you need from a technical analysis standpoint to determine whether a market is trending or sideways. The biggest thing to remember is when you do not have a strong trending market; you have the ideal conditions for writing a covered call.

Bollinger Bands

Bollinger bands are a fantastic indicator because they can be used to measure the degree of volatility in a stock's price. They're plotted over price bars, and this removes the need for you to take a look at another window when trying to interpret them. The bands themselves are constructed using prior price action.

Figure 7: Bollinger Bands on Wal-Mart

There are three curves that constitute the Bollinger Bands. In the middle of the envelope is the 20 days Exponential Moving Average (EMA) of the price. This is the average of the prior 20 values that Wal-Mart stock closed at. The curves above and below the EMA are two standard deviations away from it.

The idea is that a price move that is more than two standard deviations away from the average price movement is an extraordinary one. A move to such extremes will almost always result in a pullback towards the mean. This is because 2 standard deviations represent a

95% chance of prices being between the bands rather than outside them. From the chart, you can see how Wal-Mart pulls back towards the center every time it hits one of the outer envelopes. The only exception is when it enters a strong trend. In that case prices stick to the envelopes for a lot longer.

While this is a great trading strategy by itself, it isn't the one we're interested in. Since our objective is to write options on Wal-Mart, what we're concerned with is volatility. The Bollinger Bands give us a great way to measure this visually. Notice that the bands contract and expand as price moves from left to right.

A contraction of the band represents a narrower range that prices are trading in. In the area indicated by the ellipse on the left of Figure 7, you will notice how the bands expanded when Wal-Mart moved into a decent uptrend. Also notice how the bands visually squeezed before moving apart.

The squeeze is something that many traders use to time moves in the markets. Once the bands move close to one another, traders anticipate a strong move in some direction to occur eventually. The bands don't provide directional guidance, but they do alert the trader that a strong move might arrive shortly. Notice the portion of the chart represented by the rectangle. Here the bands are close to one another. You would have immediately known that Wal-Mart is moving in a small range.

Also notice how the bands keep coming close to one another. Like a coiled spring that is released, the stock then jumps up massively before declining to erase close to three quarters of the gains. The objective here isn't to predict this up and down movement. As a trader, when you see the bands continuously squeeze, you can be sure that an explosion is coming.

Therefore, write your calls at a farther distance than usual. If you see bands that are wide, you'll know that a trend is on and you'll write your calls far away by default. Bollinger Bands prevent you from falling into the trap that many new traders walk right into. They see a tight sideways move and try to capture the high premiums on the calls that are closer to the money.

The result is that they get taken out by the market's upward swing and lose their long position as a result. This is not a bad thing if you're a short-term trader. In such cases you can actively target band squeezes and write calls close to the money. This way you'll increase your chances of capturing gains on the stock leg as well as on the option leg.

Parabolic SAR

SAR stands for *stop and reverse,* and it's a pretty apt description of this indicator. The SAR is plotted on the price chart itself as a series of dots. When the dots are plotted above price, it's a short indication. When they're below price, it's time to go long.

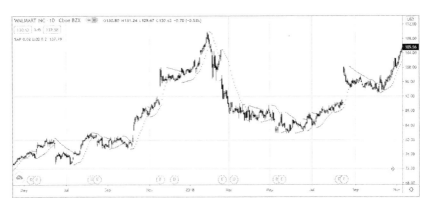

Figure 8: Parabolic SAR on Wal-Mart

In this chart you can see Wal-Mart on a strong uptrend followed by a strong downtrend, which then reverses into an uptrend once again. In short, this sort of a chart is a nightmare for most traders to profit from. It's extremely volatile and predicting short-term directions is tough.

The SAR makes your life a lot easier when it comes to this. It doesn't work very well in sideways markets as you can see towards the left of the chart. The dots alternate very quickly and it isn't enough time for you to predict the direction. However, as a covered call writer, you can easily ride out such moves because you have at least a month's holding time.

If you spot a dots pattern that alternate in quick succession, you can risk a closer call. However, if you see dots constantly printing on one side of price, especially at the bottom, you'll need to push your calls out further. The great thing about the SAR is that you don't need to evaluate any numbers. It's as simple as looking at the dots and making a decision.

You can combine this with the Bollinger Bands for greater effectiveness. However, it's best to keep your system as simple as possible. Explore one indicator and notice how it moves. Add layers on top of it once you're comfortable making money on it.

This covers our quick introduction to technical analysis, in the next chapter, we will build upon this with stock charts and demonstrate how easy it is to find great stocks for covered call writing.

Note: If you do want to dive deeper into the world of technical analysis, there are three additional books we recommend.

The first is *Technical Analysis Explained* by Martin Pring, which is often referred to as the "Bible" of technical analysis. The second, which focuses more on candlestick patterns, is *Japanese Candlestick Charting Techniques* by Steve Nison.

If you want a shorter read, which goes beyond just using technical analysis for covered calls, but is more in line with our own views, then the aptly named *Technical Analysis is Mostly Bullsh*t* by Tim Morris is worth a look as well.

9

A SIMPLE METHOD FOR SELECTING THE RIGHT STOCKS TO WRITE COVERED CALLS ON

How should you go about selecting the right stocks to write covered calls on? Once again, the answer to this question depends on the reasons you wish to enter the long stock leg of the trade.

As we've mentioned before, the best scenario would be for you to enter the long stock leg for investment purposes. Discussing the correct process of long term stock investing is something we've covered in our other books, particularly *The 8 Step Beginner's Guide to Value Investing*. If you're interested in learning all about the correct method of investing in stocks, we highly recommend you read that book in addition to this one. You'll learn the ins and outs of the Freeman investment approach and will learn the right principles to successfully invest your money.

In this chapter we're going to deal with the scenario where you're looking for stocks to earn a short-term profit using covered calls.

STABILITY

Stability is an important quality you must look for when writing covered calls. You don't want to be writing covered calls against penny stocks that can increase by 1,000% and decline by the same amount. Other stocks to avoid are hot stocks that are being discussed in the media or are present in sectors that attract many speculators.

Some examples include stocks such as Tesla and Apple in mid 2020 or marijuana companies in late 2017 to early 2018. Everyone piles into these stocks, making their volatility extremely high. This makes covered call writing less than profitable because it limits the upside of your long stock holding by nature.

Therefore the ideal covered call writing candidate is a boring stock that you would be thrilled to own for the long term.

Ideally, it pays a dividend, so your profits will be boosted by the income you earn from the call premiums. These stocks should not be sexy or high-growth in any way. An excellent example of this is Coca-Cola. Everyone knows what to expect from this company. It'll earn money, it'll earn enough to reinvest into keeping its business running, and it will earn enough to pay a steady dividend. Its stock price reflects this and rarely does anything out of the ordinary. Here are some other criteria for you to screen for.

Gently Rising Profits and Revenues

When choosing covered call candidates, you want to choose companies that have a good record of profitability but not those that are expected to increase exponentially anytime soon. This is why it's best to start off choosing large or mega-cap companies. Amazon and other tech companies are an exception to this rule since no one knows how large tech will become at this point. Amazon is a mega-cap company but is still arguably growing.

You want to choose well established businesses that have simple business structures. We highlighted Coca-Cola as an example. Ford is another example. This company has never sought a bailout, unlike its rivals, and isn't ever talked about in the hot stock news like Tesla and other electric car companies. Ford can release a fully electric line of cars should they choose to, so it isn't as if the company is behind the curve. AT&T is another example of a stock that has historically been a solid covered call candidate.

These companies are predictable and their stock prices aren't going to shoot in one particular direction. On top of this, even if their prices decline, you'll be more than happy to own them for the long term.

Low Debt

The objective of covered call writing is to generate free leverage for yourself. Leverage is something that boosts your gains immensely. The problem is that debt-based leverage can cause as much harm as the good it creates. When it comes to company finances, a leveraged balance sheet will cause the equity value to jump around.

This translates to excessive volatility in the stock price, and this is a bad thing for covered call writing. You'll never know when the price will rise. Even worse, it could fall dramatically and leave you holding onto a stock that is too unpredictable. Look for companies with very low debt to equity ratios and note the trend of this ratio. The optimal ratio varies from industry to industry, but in general, you want to look for companies with a debt to equity ratio of less than 2. Equally as important, we want the trend to be declining, meaning the company has less debt on its books year after year.

Sector and Age

It's best to stick to companies that are at least five years old and are operating in sectors that aren't prone to exogenous shocks. This means cyclical sectors such as travel, real estate, basic materials, and airlines are out. For this reason, we also stay away from writing covered calls on commodities and commodity ETFs.

Sticking to older companies also assures you that the management is well-versed in dealing with shocks to their industry. FedEx and UPS might be considered boring companies, but they're run by stable management teams that have handled multiple issues in their sector. Look for companies that largely promote from within and don't bring outside CEOs on board.

This hints at a stable corporate culture that rewards commitment to the business. As a result, the management knows the business inside and out and you'll be more than safe holding onto their stock.

Trading Volumes

Stick to companies that trade an average of over a million shares daily. This ensures no one can corner the stock in the short term and manipulate the markets. Market manipulation typically happens with penny stocks where large promoters buy the stock and pump prices up to squeeze shorts.

Dividend Yields and Payouts

It isn't necessary for you to insist on companies that pay dividends, but you can still consider them. Dividend-paying companies have a history of stability and you'll know for sure that the company is stable and in a predictable business. A company such as AT&T is a fantastic candidate to write covered calls against because the stock's current dividend yield is around 7%, which drives your potential gains even higher.

One thing to note is how long a company has been paying dividends because this can act as a proxy for stability. In fact, there are publicly traded companies that have *increased* their dividend payouts every year for the past 50 years. To find a list of these companies, you can search online for Dividend Kings, which have increased dividends every year for the past 50 years, or Dividend Aristocrats (companies who have increased dividends every year for the past 25 years).

You could choose companies that pay high dividend yields (the percentage a company pays out in dividends relative to its stock price), but don't chase yields just for the sake of them. These companies are typically in a declining business and their previous payouts are high compared to their currently depressed stock price. Thus, the high yield is artificial. Also stay away from companies that have a high payout ratio. Stick to large companies that are paying out less than 40% of their net profits on average over the past decade.

Implied Volatility

Look for stocks that are trading at implied volatility levels between 30 and 70. We'll explain implied volatility in more detail shortly. For now, just keep these numbers in mind.

No Upcoming Special Events

The stock in question must not have any major events taking place anytime soon. The most notable of these for any company is an earnings announcement. Earnings announcements tend to increase volatility in a stock and make them unpredictable. This is especially the case if there's an earnings announcement close to the option expiry date. The option's price will be inflated, which makes it likely that the stock might start jumping around too much for your comfort.

When writing index options or on ETFs that track indices, stay away from writing them during times when events that could cause a lot of volatility in the markets occur. For example, don't write calls during the month of the presidential elections or significant world events which have the power to sway an entire index one way or another.

FINDING QUALITY COVERED CALLS STOCKS FOR FREE USING SCREENING SOFTWARE

Using stock screeners is a great way to save time finding stocks that qualify according to this criteria. You might think that most screeners are expensive, but the fact is that many free screeners are more than capable of doing the job. One particular screener that we recommend using is Finviz, because the free version has everything you need to screen for covered call candidates.

Figure 9: The basic Finviz.com screener using the free version of Finviz

Here are the screening criteria you need to input into the software to find suitable candidate:

- Optionable (this just means you can buy/sell options on the stock)
- Dividend Yield over two percent (to act as a proxy for company stability, and to earn extra premium if we're holding the stock when it goes ex-dividend)
- Over one million shares traded daily (to satisfy our volume requirements)
- Earnings reported in the previous week (so there is no earnings season to deal with - on the paid version of Finviz you can customize this field and use larger time frames such as the previous 30 days)
- Price under $50 (not a necessity, but this assumes you have a small account to begin with - remember that you need to purchase a minimum of 100 shares to write a covered call)

There are many stocks that will be thrown up from this screen. Often more than 50, which fit all of these criteria. Once this is done, you can proceed to analyze their charts to determine whether they're good candidates to implement a covered call strategy.

Note: If you want to see a video of how to set this up on the Finviz website, then we have an entire series of "Covered Call Basics" for free on our YouTube channel, which you can find by going to

https://freemanpublications.com/youtube

The most important thing to remember is that you want to avoid stocks that look like they might decline in price. This is the case only when you're looking to enter for a short period of time. It doesn't apply to situations where you're looking to hold onto the stock for a long period, as we explained at the start of this chapter. When you look at charts to determine covered call candidates, look for the ones that are headed into a potential uptrend.

FREEMAN COVERED CALL RULE #9

NEVER SELL COVERED CALLS
ON A STOCK WHICH IS ON A DOWN TREND

A way you can use the technical analysis capabilities of Finviz to help you with this is to go to the "Technical" tab and select stocks that are trading above their 50-day moving average. This will give you those stocks that are more bullish than neutral, and will increase your chances of being profitable.

We'll now present four candidates to analyze for covered call suitability. Our screen was run in August 2020 and all information is given as of that month. We will present the following trade ideas:

- Two companies that could be good covered call writing candidates

- One trade idea where you can possibly make money through call option premiums, but the call option you wrote has a high likelihood of being assigned. So you would have to sell 100 shares of that particular stock
- Two companies which would be unsuitable for covered call writing
- One trade idea where you will receive call option premiums, but with the probability that the call options received will not cover the possible losses of the 100 shares of stock with declining prices

Solid Candidate 1: Morgan Stanley (NYSE:MS)

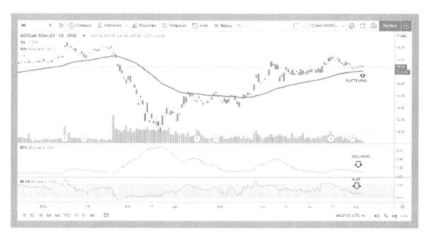

Figure 10: The daily price chart of Morgan Stanley

This chart shows the price action of Morgan Stanley (MS). The thick red line represents the 50-day Exponential Moving Average (50EMA) indicator we used in the screening section to look for stocks on a more bullish trend. Because the current price of MS is above the 50EMA, and the 50EMA is currently flattening, after rising since May 2020, this indicates that the current price of MS will probably trade within the USD44-54 range like it has been since June

Right below the main price chart is the Bollinger Band Width and the Bollinger Band %B indicators. These two indicators are derived from the Bollinger Band indicator, which indicates the probability that a stock would enter either a trending or a consolidation (sideways) phase.

As we mentioned before, Bollinger Bands move like a rubber band. If the stock trends (up or down), the bands stretch, with the Bollinger Band Width and %B increasing in value. If the stock begins flattening, then the Bollinger Band Width and %B declines in value, indicating a shift in stock price action, from trending to a consolidation phase.

In Figure 8, the Bollinger Band Width is below .20 and it is currently declining, which gives us the probability that MS will stay in the USD44-54 range. The Bollinger Band %B is currently flat, which also gives us the probability that MS will stay in the USD44-54 range.

As far as the covered call goes, the best strike price which fits our analysis is the September 18, 2020 $52.50 call option, which had 42 days left to expiry at the time of writing. This strike price has only a 26.91% chance of being in the money, and for one contract, you could receive premiums of USD111.00 (minus commissions).

Solid Candidate 2: Pfizer (NYSE:PFE)

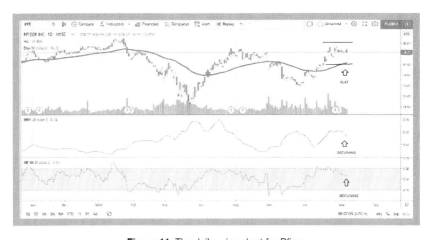

Figure 11: The daily price chart for Pfizer

This chart shows the price action of Pfizer (PFE). The current price of PFE is above the 50EMA, with the 50EMA currently flattening, after rising since July 2020. This gives us the probability that the current price of PFE will be trading within the USD36-40 range.

Like the previous chart with Morgan Stanley, the Bollinger Band Width is below .20, and it is currently declining, which gives us the probability that PFE will stay in the USD36-40 range. The Bollinger Band %B is currently declining, which also gives us the probability that PFE will stay in the USD36-40 range.

There is a September 18, 2020 $40 call option which has a strike price with only a 29.74% chance of being in the money. For contract, you could receive premiums of USD70.00 (less commissions).

Poor Candidate 1: Bank of America (NYSE:BAC)

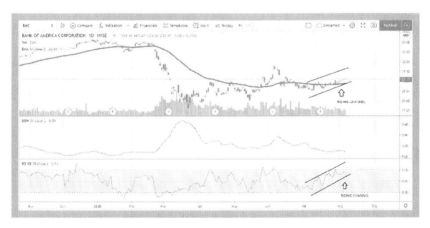

Figure 12: The daily price chart of Bank of America

Figure 12 and the next chart are examples of stocks that are not good candidates for writing covered calls. Figure 12 shows the price action of Bank of America (BAC). The current price of BAC is above the 50EMA, and the 50EMA currently flat. However, the price of BAC is currently inside a rising channel, signifying an uptrend is in progress.

The Bollinger Band Width is below .20, and it is currently flat. The Bollinger Band %B, however, is currently in a rising channel, which gives us the probability that BAC will have higher prices in the next 30-45 days.

BAC is not a good covered call writing candidate at this time, since the price of BAC will increase in the next 30-45 days, which presents the probability that the call option we wrote will be assigned, forcing us to sell the 100 shares of BAC.

Poor Candidate 2: Western Union (NYSE:WU)

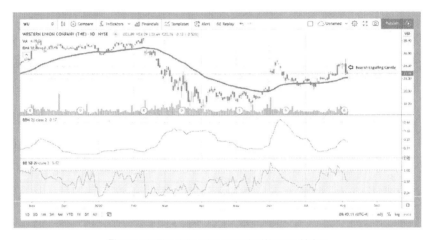

Figure 13: The daily price chart for Western Union

This chart shows the price action of Western Union (WU). The current price of WU is above the 50EMA, with the 50EMA currently rising.

However, WU's price is expected to decline, as the chart of $WU showed a big, bearish, engulfing pattern when its earnings report was released August 4, 2020.

This shows that WU is not a good covered call writing candidate at this time, since we expect the price of WU to decline in the next 30-45 days. This gives us the probability that the call options premium collected will be less than the losses to be incurred in the 100 shares of stock, making this particular covered call option idea futile.

THE ROLE OF IMPLIED
VOLATILITY IN COVERED CALLS

When trading options, there are three types of volatility you need to take into account. The first is the overall market volatility. This is measured by the volatility index, or VIX. The VIX is an index maintained by the CBOE and lists the current volatility in the market. This is particularly useful if you're looking to trade index options.

When it comes to individual stocks, though, the VIX isn't of much use. This is because every stock has its own volatility characteristics, and the overall market doesn't affect it too much. Each stock has its own following amongst traders and in the short term, this causes stock behavior to diverge from the market's overall behavior.

When it comes to an individual stock, there are two types of volatility to take into account. The first is historical volatility or beta. Beta is a measure of how much the stock moved around in the past compared to the index. Which ain't all that important when it comes to determining the viability of writing a covered call. As covered call writers, what's far more important to us is the implied volatility of the stock we're writing the call against. Let's look at this in more detail.

IMPLIED VOLATILITY

A stock's implied volatility is a forward projection of how much the market expects the stock to move, given all of the future events and considerations that are known at this point. For example, if the market recognizes that an upcoming earnings announcement might create volatility in the stock price, the implied volatility on its options will be high.

The closer an option is to expiry, the lower its implied volatility will be. This is because the underlying price moves have less chance of impacting the price of the option. Much like the time value of an option, the implied volatility will decrease as an option moves closer to expiry. However, this isn't always the case.

If the market expects a piece of news to create significant volatility, and if this event occurs before expiry, then the option's implied volatility will not decrease as much. Implied volatility is a key component of the Black-Scholes model which is the formula that is used to calculate the fair price of an option. It plays a significant role in the final value that is determined by this formula.

The first thought that most covered call writers have is that they ought to target options with low implied volatility. This makes sense since you want stocks that are in moderately bullish conditions or those that are moving sideways. However, do note that implied volatility doesn't indicate direction. It only indicates how forcefully you can expect the stock to move.

Secondly, a low implied volatility reduces the price of the option. This means the premium you earn on writing it will be low and this reduces your returns. Over a long-enough time period you'll end up making less money by targeting these options.

Figure 14 illustrates the impact that implied volatility has on the option premium.

$120 calls for Disney (3 strikes OTM) trading at $116.18

Expiry Date	DTE	IV	Option Premium	CC Yield	News
8/8/2020	9	43.53%	1.78	1.53%	Earnings (Aug 4)
8/15/2020	16	39.06%	2.36	2.03%	
8/22/2020	23	36.77%	2.65	2.28%	
8/29/2020	30	35.51%	3.15	2.71%	
9/5/2020	37	34.83%	3.50	3.01%	
9/19/2020	51	32.29%	4.03	3.47%	
10/16/2020	79	33.14%	5.35	4.60%	
1/15/2021	170	33.25%	8.55	7.36%	Earnings (Nov 5)

$13 calls for American Airlines (3 strikes OTM), trading at $11.77

Expiry Date	DTE	IV	Option Premium	CC Yield	News
8/8/2020	9	87.89%	0.26	2.2%	
8/15/2020	16	84.57%	0.29	2.5%	
8/22/2020	23	87.80%	0.6	5.1%	
8/29/2020	30	92.38%	0.73	6.2%	
9/5/2020	37	83.40%	0.92	7.8%	
9/19/2020	51	88.57%	1.12	9.5%	
10/16/2020	79	102.34%	1.58	13.4%	Earnings (Oct 22)
1/15/2021	170	97.46%	2.67	22.7%	

Figure 14: The relationship between IV and covered call yield (option premium divided by the price of underlying)

As you can see, there is a higher yield for the higher IV options on American Airlines, but this comes with additional risk. You don't know which way volatility might push prices. It could go up or down. Notice that in the case of Disney, the January options have a high IV. This month's options contracts have both a large time value as well as implied volatility built into them. This is what results in the high contract price. However, if the earnings announcement goes pear-shaped for Disney, covered call writers will be left owning a stock position that has large capital losses.

When looking at implied volatility, choose options that are between 30 to 70%. Contracts that are below 30 won't give you enough premium, and those above 70 will be far too volatile and might go the other way, leaving you with a large capital loss.

It is even possible for stocks to have an implied volatility greater than 100%. This generally happens for two reasons. The first is with deep ITM and deep OTM strikes close to expiration where only an extreme event could result in an unexpected outcome. The second is for cases where the company share price hinges solely on one key piece of news, such as the result of a drug trial for a biotech company. Avoid stocks where this is the case, because covered calls limit your upside by design. If you're writing calls on stocks with an IV over 100, you're exposing yourself to higher risk without being able to capture the higher reward.

FREEMAN COVERED CALL RULE #10

STICK TO WRITING COVERED CALLS ON STOCKS
WITH AN IMPLIED VOLATILITY OF
BETWEEN 30 AND 70

11

A RELIABLE METHOD FOR SELECTING THE CORRECT STRIKE PRICES

How should you go about selecting the right strike prices? In order to understand the answer to this question better, we need to first begin with the reason an investor enters the long stock leg of the trade. Investors can enter either for long-term investment purposes or for short-term profits.

If you are entering for the long term, you want to choose strikes that are far enough away so that the option finishes OTM, and your long stock position doesn't get called away. You also want the option at that strike price to have enough of a premium so that you earn a decent level of cash flow income on your investment.

If you have a short-term bias, on the other hand, you'll looking for your call to finish in the money. Your objective is to be able to capture both the capital gains in the stock as well as earn a decent option premium. When executed well, the returns on this strategy are enormous.

Central to both strategies' success is choosing the right strike price. In order to understand how to choose the right strike price, we need to dive into the world of the Greeks.

The Greeks are five variables that measure different aspects of an options contract. You don't need to learn about all of them, and in fact, there are just two (delta and theta), which are most relevant to covered call writing. So providing you have a basic understanding of what these two Greeks represent, then you'll have more than enough knowledge to make profitable trades consistently.

DELTA

When it comes to covered call writing, the most important Greek to understand is delta. Delta (Δ) is the ratio that measures the change in the price of an asset to the corresponding change in the option connected to the asset. When writing covered calls, we use delta to help us choose optimal strike prices.

An option with a delta value of 0.5 will increase by $0.50 for every dollar's increase in the share price, assuming there are no special events to account for. These values can be positive or negative and this depends on the option type. Call deltas are always positive and range from 0 to 1. This is because as prices increase, the value of a call option increases. Put deltas are negative and range from 0 to -1 since the value of a put option increases as the stock's value decreases.

Delta values are designed to be read as percentages, and in some instances you will see them represented as such. For example, if you see a delta of 30% this is equivalent to a delta of 0.3. It indicates that the option will increase in a value equivalent to 30% of the overall increase in the stock's price. In the case of a put, a decrease in stock price will produce the equivalent percentage change.

Like implied volatility, delta is a key input to the Black-Scholes model. You don't need to understand how it works, as long as you know that delta helps us understand how option prices ought to vary depending on the price of the stock. Delta is particularly useful since it is extremely predictable and is often used by professional options portfolio managers.

A call option's delta depends on where the underlying price is relative to the strike price. Options that are ITM are usually pretty close to 1, while OTM options are closer to 0. The closer an option is ITM, the higher the delta values are. An ATM option usually has a delta of around 0.5.

The interesting thing about delta is that it is used as a proxy to determine how likely an option is to finish ITM. There isn't a direct correlation between the price change of an option and its probability of finishing ITM, all things remaining the same, but traders have observed that delta is a pretty good substitute for this. This is where the key to picking correct strike prices lies.

PICKING STRIKE PRICES

CALLS							**STRIKE**
BID x ASK	VOLUME OPTN OPN I...	DELTA	GAMMA	VEGA	THETA		
• 4.55 x 4.70 •	8	0.961	0.029	0.007	-0.005		25
• 4.05 x 4.25 •		0.950	0.037	0.009	-0.006		25.5
• 3.60 x 3.75 •		0.936	0.048	0.010	-0.007		26
• 3.10 x 3.30 •		0.919	0.063	0.013	-0.007		26.5
• 2.67 x 2.76 •	3	0.889	0.083	0.016	-0.009		27
• 2.23 x 2.31 •	2	0.848	0.108	0.020	-0.010		27.5
• 1.83 x 1.89 •	153	0.794	0.137	0.024	-0.012		28
• 1.40 x 1.49 •	17	0.722	0.168	0.028	-0.013		28.5
• 1.10 x 1.15 •	76	0.633	0.194	0.030	-0.014		29
• 0.79 x 0.84 •	187	0.532	0.211	0.032	-0.015		29.5
• 0.58 x 0.60 •	2.36K	0.426	0.211	0.031	-0.014		30
• 0.37 x 0.43 •	282	0.326	0.195	0.029	-0.013		30.5
• 0.26 x 0.30 •	1.12K	0.239	0.168	0.026	-0.011		31
• 0.16 x 0.18 •	267	0.168	0.135	0.022	-0.009		31.5
• 0.12 x 0.13 •	13.5K	0.122	0.105	0.018	-0.007		32
• 0.06 x 0.10 •	39	0.086	0.079	0.015	-0.006		32.5
• 0.06 x 0.07 •	344	0.065	0.061	0.011	-0.005		33
• 0.03 x 0.06 •	103	0.046	0.045	0.008	-0.004		33.5
• 0.03 x 0.04 •	69	0.035	0.035	0.006	-0.003		34
• 0.02 x 0.04 •	25	0.025	0.025	0.006	-0.002		34.5

Figure 15: The call side options prices for AT&T with 26 days left to expiry
(Source: Interactive Brokers)

Figure 15 shows the option chain for AT&T, which was trading at $29.57 at the time of this writing. The strike prices are listed in the extreme right-hand column, while delta is listed with the other Greeks in the columns to its left.

Notice that the 25 strike price has a delta of 0.961. Which means for every $1, the stock price increases, the price of the 25 call option will increase by $0.961. This makes sense since it is deep in the money. Based on what we said above about delta being a proxy for the probability this particular strike will finish ITM, you can interpret this situation as the 25 strike AT&T call has a 96.1% chance of finishing in the money.

At this point, many traders will run away and start writing ITM options since these have a good probability of finishing in the money. However, this isn't a good idea for two reasons.

The first is that deep ITM options have barely any extrinsic value to them. This means the entire value of the option is intrinsic, and thus you are barely receiving a premium as the writer. The second is that your option will nearly always be exercised, and you'll have to sell the stock at much lower than the market price, which means you don't benefit from any upside price movement.

Writing ATM options isn't intelligent either since you'll be relying on just the option premium income. This doesn't suit the long-term investor's needs either, so for covered call writing, writing ATM or ITM options isn't a very smart thing to do.

The point here isn't to pick the strike with the highest delta. It's to pick the strike that is OTM and has a reasonable chance of finishing ITM. That's what makes you a ton of money, because you can collect the premium from writing the strike *and* benefit from the capital gains if the stock price increases.

Using the option chain in the table above for AT&T, let's say we choose to write the option with a strike price of $30. This is quite close to the current price of $29.57 and the delta reflects this. Remember, an ITM option has a delta of greater than 0.5. The delta for the 30 strike is currently .426. This means it has a 42.6% chance of finishing ITM.

Once this happens, you have a decent chance of the underlying being called away, and this leaves you with a profit of 43 cents per share. You'll also earn the option premium which is $0.60 per share. Here is how the numbers work on this trade:

Cost of entry = Cost of buying 100 shares of AT&T at current market price = $2,957
Premium earned on writing 30 strike call = $60
If option finishes ITM, profit = Profit on stock sale + Premium earned = ($43 + $49) = $92
Percent return = 3.1%

Remember that this is the return you'll receive for a trade which lasts just 26 days. Because you'll be writing options that will expire 45 days away at most, if you could replicate this return over the course of a year, you'll earn an annualized return of 37.3%. That is a massive return for a stable stock which isn't appreciating much.

You'll have to take commissions into account, of course, but these days many brokers don't charge traders any commissions on options trading. Some don't even charge commissions on assignment or exercise. Assuming this is the case, short-term capital gains taxes are your only expense. These come out of your profits, so it's not as if it's a massive hit.

In the case of the long-term investor who wishes to hang onto their stock investment, choosing a strike with a delta that is as close to zero as possible is the smart thing to do. Referring to the table in Figure 15, we can choose the 34.50 call, which has a delta of 0.025. This is effectively telling us that this option has a 2.5% chance of finishing in the money, assuming all things remain the same and that no volatility shock occurs.

The premium you'll earn from writing this option is 0.04 per share. This is $4 per contract. This is a yield of 0.13% on the current market price, which isn't much. However, it's a monthly yield. Multiply this by 12 and you'll realize a 1.6% yield by writing these OTM options.

Remember that if you're going to be a long-term investor, you'll be earning dividends on your stock ownership as well. AT&T's dividend currently yields around 7%. This means you're guaranteeing a return of over 8% percent every year (the stock dividend + the deep OTM call yields), whether the market goes up or down or does nothing. This is before any long-term capital gains that the stock gives you.

Then there's also the fact that you can reinvest these gains into the stock to have them compound at the average capital gains rate. We've already highlighted the benefits of doing this and have shown how you can double your money compared to relying solely on capital gains.

As a rule of thumb, if you're looking for extra income from your covered calls, you want to be picking deltas that are as close to 40% as possible. In the AT&T example, we have two deltas that are at 43% and 32%. Picking the 43% delta makes more sense since this is more likely to finish ITM. Long-term investors can pick the lowest delta that still gives you a satisfactory return on your money.

FREEMAN COVERED CALL RULE #11

IF YOU WANT TO CAPTURE A GOOD PREMIUM, AND
RETAIN YOUR LONG STOCK
HOLDINGS, PICK THE STRIKE PRICE WITH A DELTA
AS CLOSE TO 0.4 (40%) AS POSSIBLE

Conservative investors can choose the delta that is as low as possible almost to guarantee a return on their money. Remember that the delta percentage is not a 100% guarantee. There could be volatility shocks to the market that will cause everything to be thrown out of order. This is just one of the risks of investing.

THE SIMPLE SOLUTION FOR CHOOSING EXPIRY DATES

L ike with strike prices, choosing the correct expiry dates for your options is critical. Choose the wrong expiry date, and you could be leaving money on the table. This happens because of the way time decay works. We've already explained how a significant portion of an option's premium is its time value.

The time value inherent in an option's price is a measure of the option's likelihood of moving into the money. The more time there is until option expiry, the higher the likelihood of the option moving into the money. This increases the time value in the price of the option.

Here is the golden rule, as an option seller, time decay is your friend. You want the option to expire worthless if you're a long-term investor who wishes to hang onto your long stock position. For short-term traders, the decline in the time value needs to be balanced with the fact that you also want to ensure your option finishes in the money so that you can collect your profit plus the premium.

For short-term traders, choosing the expiry date is a tricky proposition. On one hand the longer term options give you maximum time value, but you also need to make sure that your option has a good chance of being assigned to you. This means you want it to finish deep in the money or at the money upon expiry, at the very least. Some covered call traders bank on early exercise, but this is a mistake.

There is no guarantee your option will be exercised early. In fact, the majority of options are not exercised early. The final week prior to expiry is when most options are exercised since there's very little time value left in them, and most buyers have nothing to gain by hanging onto them.

One important thing to note is that time decay is not linear. Time decay (also known as *theta decay* using Greek terminology) accelerates once the option moves within 30 days of expiry. This means the best time frame for you to target when it comes to expiry dates for covered calls is the 30-45 day window. This will give you enough of a window where you can reasonably predict price movements, and you'll earn a good return as well, thanks to the in-built time value in the premium.

WHEN SHOULD YOU CHOOSE LONGER-TERM OPTIONS?

Some traders might prefer choosing longer-term options since this suits their psyche better. A lot of long-term investors adopt this set and forget approach. While a covered call cannot guarantee that you can forget about your trade, the degree to which you must monitor your trade doesn't change or depend on the expiry date.

If anything, you'll be monitoring your trade to the same degree as you usually would. The only time when a longer expiry date makes sense is if the time premium results in a prorated gain that is far higher than what a monthly option would provide you with. For example, if the premium on a call that is expiring in 30 days gives you a 1.5% yield and one that is expiring two months from now gives you a 3% yield, it doesn't make sense to write the longer term option.

On a monthly basis, both yields are the same. If the longer-term option gives you a greater yield, then opt for it. Take the deltas into account as well. Typically, the longer-term options will have a higher delta than the shorter-term ones. Longer-term options also give you greater opportunities to capture higher capital gains in your investment since the stock has a greater opportunity to rise to higher levels.

Those who wish to hold onto the stock leg for investment purposes should not choose long expiry terms. This is because the yield you will earn on longer-term options will be lower than writing short-term ones. Besides, having a long-term option position will only increase the risk of your stock being called away.

What if you want to get rid of your stock, but don't want to write an ITM option? In such cases you need first to ask yourself why you wish to let go of your stock position.

Sometimes, you realize that there are no significant capital gains on your stock investments and you decide to start collecting income. If the stock you're holding isn't going to be heading upwards anytime soon, and if you wish to invest your money in something else, your best move is to let that investment go instead of trying to squeeze a few yield points from it.

You could write a call that is close to the money in the hopes of it being called away. However, the risk here is that if the stock is indeed going to run into turbulent times, and if your original reason for investing in it isn't valid anymore, you'll face the possibility of far greater capital gains or losses than whatever income you manage to earn. This is something a lot of covered call writers forget.

As great as the additional points of yield are, they pale in comparison to capital gains. Imagine that you buy a stock worth $100. A $1 rise in prices gives you a one percent gain. This isn't such an outlandish rise. However, with covered calls, you'll need to write calls all year to earn around four to five percent if you're being conservative.

A stock can cover a 4-5% rise in a few days, let alone weeks. The only disadvantage with capital gains is that they're unrealized and this is why generating cash flow is so valuable. However, don't make the mistake of minimizing the importance of strong capital gains in your investment. That's what makes you money at the end of the day.

So take this into account if you're a long-term investor. If there's even the slightest chance of your capital gains reducing, sell your stock position as quickly as you can. If the stock is merely going to move sideways, then you can afford to collect some additional cash on the position. Write calls close to the money and maximize your yield on exit.

WATCH OUT FOR EVENTS IN YOUR OPTION HOLDING PERIOD

When selecting an expiry date, make sure there are no significant events such as earnings announcements or political events coming up as mentioned previously. These affect the volatility and make it tough for you to predict where the underlying will end. This is why we used the "earnings in the previous week" filter on Finviz, because earnings announcements are the most frequent event that significantly affects a company's stock price.

FREEMAN COVERED CALL RULE #12

ENSURE THERE ARE NO MAJOR EVENTS WHICH
COULD AFFECT THE PRICE OF THE
STOCK DURING THE PERIOD YOU HOLD YOUR
OPTIONS CONTRACT

13

CALCULATING RETURN ON YOUR INVESTMENT

A s with any investment, you need to track the returns you're earning. This will help you measure the strategy's effectiveness and, more importantly, it'll help you avoid incurring opportunity costs. Most investors don't take this into account and end up sticking to tired old strategies that don't make them any money. In this situation, you can invest your money in other strategies that could make you more money. The gains that you forego are the opportunity costs.

Calculating the returns from your covered call position is pretty straightforward. However, the ROI can have some variations based on where the stock or the underlying asset closes on expiration.

STOCK EXPIRES AT OR SLIGHTLY BELOW THE STRIKE PRICE

To calculate the return of your covered call positions, you simply have to divide the net premium received by the cost of your shares and then convert that figure into an annualized number.

For example, you purchased 100 shares of Disney at $125 for the total investment of $12,500 and sold the $128 OTM call option expiring in one month (30 days). In return, you received $3.75 as premium and at the time of expiry the stock expires at or slightly below the strike price of $128.

In the above scenario, your total ROI on the covered call position is:

= ($375/$12,500)*100 = 3%

Afterwards, to convert this figure into an annualized return, you just simply have to take that 3% and multiply it by 365, divided by the number of days left for expiration from the date of entry.

Annualized Rate of Return:

= Rate of return on the existing covered call position * 365/ Number of days left
for expiration
= 3*365/30
= 36.50%

STOCK EXPIRES ABOVE THE STRIKE PRICE

The above example was quite straightforward because your income was restricted only to the premium received from selling the call options. However, in certain scenarios, stock prices expire above the strike price. In such a case, calculating ROI is quite different.

Continuing with the above example, let's assume the stock price expires at $130 (above the strike price) at the time of expiration.

In such a scenario, your return from the premium received will remain the same at 36.5%. But, the stock will be called away. Meaning, you are now obligated to sell the stock at $128 for $300 [($128 - $125)*100] in realized capital gains.

In the above scenario, your total ROI on the covered calls position is:

($375 + $300)/12,500 = 5.4%

Annualized Rate of Return:

= Rate of return on the existing covered call position * 365/
Number of days left
for expiration
= 5.4*365/30
= 65.70%

STOCK EXPIRES SIGNIFICANTLY BELOW THE STRIKE PRICE

Losses are a part of trading. Learning to book these losses and keep tracking them regularly is also equally important. In case of covered calls, the risk lies in the underlying stock and not with the options. A small bearish move won't affect your overall position because you still end up making the premium amount. However, if the stock moves down significantly, it will result in a significant capital loss.

In the above example, let's say Disney gapped down the next day because of some unexpected bad news and it fell to $110. Under such circumstances, it is advisable to close the trade by selling the under-lying stock and close the short call position and book the loss. If you don't close the short call position along with the underlying stock, you would end up with a naked call position.

In the above scenario, your total ROI on the covered calls position is:

(*$11,000 + $375 - $12,000)/12,500 = -9%

*$11,000 is the net proceeds from selling the underlying stock at $110.

We must mention that if you wish to hold onto the stock position for the long term, then a falling stock price should not be of concern to you. The above advice only applies to short-term traders. Keep in mind the differences in mindset between a long-term investor and a trader.

14

COVERED CALL EXIT STRATEGIES - TAKING PROFITS VS. LETTING YOUR OPTIONS EXPIRE

W e've previously mentioned that a significant number of options contracts expire worthless, which is why we prefer to be on the writing side when it comes to options trading. A crucial part of using options successfully is making adjustments as the trade evolves. Often, trades don't automatically go your way. You'll need to decide whether you want to close the trade or adjust it to put yourself in a better position. There's a classic saying in the investing world "nobody ever went broke taking profits."

However, this doesn't mean you should take every little profit that comes your way. Doing this will result in you potentially leaving money on the table. By improving your understanding of options a little more, you can set yourself up to know exactly when to take profits and when to keep your trades open.

The first thing to do when entering any trade is to calculate the break-even price. In the case of the covered call, this is the price of your underlying stock minus the premium you received for writing the call. For example, let's say you buy AT&T at $30, and you sell a covered call with a strike at $32 with 45 days to expiry for a $1 premium. Your cost basis and break-even price for the trade is:

($30 - $1) = $29

So as long as the underlying stock price stays above $29, you are making money on the trade.

Now let's look at a few ways this trade can play out.

EXIT SCENARIO 1: STOCK MOVES UP

The first scenario is that we see a bullish move in the stock price. Let's say it's trading at $31.50, and there are four days left to expiry. If you want to realize maximum profits, you can wait and hope the option expires above $32, at which point your stock will be called away at $32 and your profit will be ($32 + $1 - $30)*100 = $300.

If you'd prefer to hold the stock long-term and don't want it to get called away if the option expires ITM above $32, you can lock in your profits by buying your call option back. This will cost you money since you'll need to pay whatever the premium is at that point. This is also called covering your short option position (the same term that's used in stock trading.)

Remember, when buying back the option, you want the option's price to be lower than the price you received upon writing it. It's a simple sell high, buy low process, and is the same as shorting a stock.

However, unlike stocks, you're almost always guaranteed a lower price as the option moves closer to expiry. This is because of the role of your friend time decay, which as we discussed earlier, is always on your side as an option seller.

Back to our example, you have just four days to expiry, and time decay has worked its magic. The price to buy back your $32 call is now just $0.10. Meaning you can pay $10 ($0.10*100) to buy back the option, locking in a profit of $90 on the option itself ($100-$10). Since you've now covered the option position, your stock will not be called away, even if the price is above $32 at expiry.

On top of this $90 realized profit, you also have unrealized gains of $150 on your 100 shares stock after the bullish move from $30 to $31.50.

EXIT SCENARIO 2: STOCK MOVES DOWNWARDS

The second scenario is if the price of the underlying has decreased after you wrote the option. Let's say the stock price is now trading at $27, and you have seven days until expiry. As you own 100 shares, your current unrealized loss is $2 per share, which is your cost basis ($29) minus the current price ($27).

Your two choices here are to either hope for a large price reversal in the next seven days or to close out the trade, then enter a new trade to further lower your cost basis. This is how many options traders adjust their trades once they discover that the position has moved against them.

Because we're closer to expiry, the price of the option has decreased due to time decay. In this case, we can buy back our $32 call option for just $0.02 because it is now far OTM. This means we've made a realized gain of $98 ($100 - $2) on that trade.

This also increases our break-even point for the stock. Remember, our original break-even point was $29. But since we bought back our option for $0.02, our new break-even point is $29.02 ($29 + the price we paid to buy back our option).

We're still holding the long stock leg of the trade, so we have an unrealized loss of $202 on it. One option we have is to continuously lower the break-even point for this leg by writing more calls and earning more premiums. This can be done by writing calls at lower strike prices.

So let's say we write a new call $30 call with 40 days to expiry for $0.60. This gives us a new cost basis of $28.42 ($29.02 - $0.60).

Now with our new lowered cost basis, if our stock rises above $28.42, the long stock position will be profitable once again.

If this new trade works in our favor and the stock finishes above $30 at expiry, we'll make $300 on the trade after the underlying is called away ($30 - $27). In addition to this, we also collected $60 in premiums from writing the second call option. Our net position is now $360 minus the $202 unrealized loss we started with. As a result, our net profits from this second trade are $158.

To summarize the P&L from both trades:

- Net premium received after buying back our call in trade 1: $98
- Unrealized capital loss after trade 1: -$202
- Premium received from entering trade 2: $60
- Realized capital gains after trade 2 ends ITM and our stock is called away: $300
- Total realized net gain after trades 1 and 2: (+$98 - $202 + $60 + $300) = $256

SCENARIO 3: STOCK DOESN'T MOVE

The final scenario is that the price doesn't change at all. Let's assume we're now five days away from expiry with the price at $30. Your first choice here is to let the option ride and wait for expiry, hoping the call option finishes OTM. This will help you keep your premium for a $100 profit.

The second choice is that you can buy back your call and lock in your profits. Thanks to time decay, the option premiums will have gotten much cheaper as we move closer to expiry. Therefore we can buy back our call for just $0.05. By doing this, we no longer have any open options contracts and are left with a profit on the trade of ($1 - $0.05)*100 or $95.

If we wanted to, we could further reduce our cost basis by then selling another call a further 42 days out at the same strike price ($32). This is called rolling out or rolling forward. You do this by writing another option that is further out in expiry. Please note that rolling out an option works differently from rolling forward other derivatives contracts. You cannot substitute an options contract for one that expires later. You need to exit the first contract and then physically enter another one.

In this case, implied volatility is slightly higher, so we collect a $1.20 premium. Remember, this further reduces our cost basis to $27.80 ($29 - $1.20).

As you can see here, writing covered calls is a fantastic way to reduce your cost basis on stocks that you plan to hold onto for the long term.

THE ROLE OF TIME DECAY IN COVERED CALL MANAGEMENT

We've mentioned time decay a few times in this chapter, so it's time to address it in depth regarding the management of your covered calls. Time decay (or *theta* Θ) is another Greek variable that appears complex on the surface but is very simple to understand once you grasp a few key concepts. It is the measure of how an option's premium is affected by time. Remember, all other factors being equal, options lose value the closer they get to expiry.

The numerical value of time decay is the measure of how much the option will lose value each day it moves closer to expiry. As the covered call is a strategy that sells options, time decay is always working in our favor. This is why our strategies involving buying back the written covered call close to expiry work since time decay makes the option premium cheaper than what it was when we first wrote it.

In terms of managing your covered calls, theta most affects strikes which are either ATM or very near the money. The further the price moves away from the strike in either direction, the lower the value of theta.

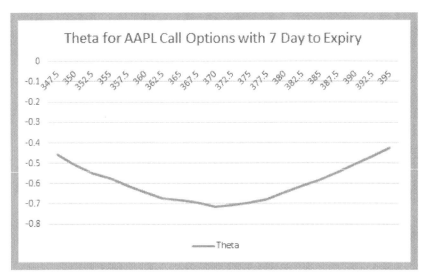

Figure 16: Theta for Apple Options with Seven Days to Expiry, Apple was trading at $370.71 at the time (Source: Interactive Brokers)

In Figure 16, the ATM strikes ($370 and $372) have the highest time decay, with theta declining as we move further away from the money. The value of theta is always negative since it represents a reduction in option premium.

Deep ITM strikes and deep OTM strikes are less affected by time decay because they have a lower likelihood of a different outcome at expiry (the OTM strike finishing ITM and vice versa).

In this way, you can think of time value as a measure of uncertainty. An analogy for this is how a football game tied at 28-28 has a more uncertain outcome with 2 minutes to go (because both teams have a good chance of winning) than a game where one team is winning 28-7 with the same time remaining.

Now that you have a better grasp of how time decay works, we can develop a practical method for using it to manage our trades. To see how we can use theta to better manage our trades, it's important to understand our options' intrinsic and extrinsic value.

Let's say we own Las Vegas Sands (LVS) currently priced at $45.00.

If we buy a $40 call for $6.50, then we have $5 of intrinsic value (because the stock is worth $5 more than the option we bought), and $1.50 of extrinsic value (the price of the option minus the intrinsic value.)

If we buy a $50 call for $1, then we have $0 of intrinsic value because the option is OTM. However, since we could resell the option for $1, it still has $1 of extrinsic value.

Because theta affects deep ITM and deep OTM strikes less, the most optimal management strategy is to roll your short calls when they are deep ITM or OTM, because you will not get a much better price by waiting to sell them closer to expiry. We'll add to this with 3 rules based exit strategies for managing your trades.

THREE RULE-BASED EXIT STRATEGIES

The One Percent Rule

A good rule to use with respect to theta decay is if the value of your call ever loses its extrinsic value to where that extrinsic value represents less than one percent of the underlying price, then roll the option over. This means buying back your existing call and selling the next month's option. A few options platforms such as *thinkorswim,* have a special "roll" functionality which will conduct both of these trades simultaneously. On other platforms, you'll need to do this manually.

If the stock moves sideways, the call option's value will decrease over time. Once the value of the call's extrinsic value is less than one percent of the stock's price, roll the call option to a new strike and expiration.

If the stock moves down, the value of the call option will drop. Once its value is less than one percent of the stock price, roll the option to a new strike and expiration.

In the Las Vegas Sands example, if the underlying price stays at $45, you should roll the option if the option price drops below $0.45, because this is now less than one percent of the underlying.

The Two and Twenty (2 & 20) Rule

We've already discussed how theta decay accelerates as your contract moves closer to the expiry date. However, what if contract prices decrease sharply during the beginning of the contract? Do you keep holding onto it in hopes of greater profit, or should you lock in your profits?

A good rule to use in such a scenario is the 2 & 20 rule. This rule states that if the price of buying back your option is less than 20% of the price you paid, within the first two weeks of you entering the contract, go ahead and buy back the option. So if you were paid a $1 premium for the contract and if it costs less than $0.20 to buy it back within the first 2 weeks, then pull the trigger and buy it back.

By doing this, you should lock in a solid profit on the contract, and you no longer have to be concerned with your stock being called away. You are giving up 20% of your potential profit by doing this, but because you've bought it back within 2 weeks of entering it, this then allows you to have the flexibility to enter into another contract if you want to do so. In essence, you're using time to your advantage by giving yourself more opportunities to enter profitable trades.

Code Red

When you spend enough time in the markets, you'll eventually enter a trade which goes pear-shaped right from the start. With covered calls, there isn't too much which can go wrong in the options leg of the trade, but there are always risks with the underlying stock.

So if you're ever in a scenario where you feel the stock itself could take a large hit in price, exit the trade at any cost and sell the underlying stock. This could be if there are allegations of fraud or if the company is under fire for its business practices.

A recent example of this would be the Muddy Waters Research report, which uncovered massive fraud at Chinese coffee company Luckin Coffee. At the time the report, which alleged that Luckin had fabricated its sales numbers, was released, the stock was trading at $32. Within 3 months the stock had fallen almost 95% and was trading below $3 and was removed from the Nasdaq as a result. However, if you had sold your stock within one month of the report being released, you would have kept the vast majority of your capital gains.

Another thing to bear in mind is not to keep holding onto the stock with the hope of making a greater profit on your options trade, because it's extremely rare that your options yields will offset the loss you made in the underlying stock.

It's an unwelcome scenario to be in, but it's best to be proactive and just get out with your capital intact and then re-enter another trade with a new stock.

This is one of the most difficult decisions for new investors and traders to make because it goes against a fundamental human desire:

the need to be right. However, once you can separate your emotions from your trading, you will be ahead of the curve and position yourself to make more money than 90% of traders out there.

FREEMAN COVERED CALL RULE #14

THERE IS NO SHAME IN
SELLING A STOCK WHICH IS
UNDERPERFORMING

15

THE POOR MAN'S COVERED CALL

As great as the covered call is, there are downsides to it. The biggest barrier to implementing it is that you need to have capital in your account to do so. For instance, if you wished to write a covered call on the SPY, which is the ETF tracking the S&P 500, you'll need at least $30,000 in your account since the ETF is selling north of $300 at the moment.

Understandably, not everyone has this kind of money lying around. What if you have just $5,000 in your account and wish to start earning some money on this? Can you still execute a covered call? The good news is that you can. Remember earlier, we discussed how options can be used to enter a position for a lower cost than simply buying stock? Well now we'll show you how to use this to execute covered calls for a lower cost than you would with a stock position. This strategy is often referred to as executing a poor man's covered call.

LONG DIAGONAL SPREADS WITH CALLS

To understand this trade better, we need to take some time to introduce some more options trading terminology. You'll often read of the word "spread" in relation to options trading. There are three kinds of spreads a trader can create. The first is a vertical spread. These spreads involve options expiring in the same month but with different strike prices.

Next is the horizontal spread, which are two options that have the same strike price but expire in different months. Usually, a horizontal spread involves one option expiring in the near month and the other expiring 30 days after that. Lastly, we have diagonal spreads that are created with calls and puts.

Diagonal spreads can be vertical or horizontal in nature. You could create a diagonal with a call and a put expiring in the same month or in different months. You can even create diagonals with calls exclusively or with puts exclusively but have them in opposite directions. We mean to say that you could have one call leg as a long position and the other as a short position.

Don't worry too much about the complexities of the diagonal spread and its structure. Of the utmost importance is that you understand why it works.

When it comes to creating a poor man's covered call, the setup is quite simple. There are two legs to a long call diagonal:

1. An ITM long call option leg with expiry out in the future, preferably a LEAP
2. An OTM short call option leg expiring within 30-45 days

LEAP stands for **L**ong-term **E**quity Antici**P**ation. These are options that expire well out into the future, usually over a year or more. The great news is that they're fully accessible to retail traders. By buying a call LEAP that expires more than a year from the current date, and one that is ITM, you've established a synthetic long position in the stock.

You can simply keep holding onto this position for a year or more and then either exit the LEAP position or exercise it to establish a long stock position. Like with regular options, each LEAP contract covers 100 shares of the underlying.

Most brokers will allow you to write covered calls against an ITM LEAP. It's still prudent to check with your broker if this is the case. These securities are available with Level 1 options accounts, the same as regular covered calls, so it shouldn't be an issue.

LEAP Substitution

The LEAP substitution strategy works best in mature bull markets. They aren't rising exponentially, and the stock you're interested in is moving slightly upwards or is moving sideways. It's best to choose a LEAP that is a year or two away in expiry. This is a big holding period, but consider that your long stock investment leg is usually held for a while as well, especially if you're using it for investment purposes.

Short-term traders can use LEAPs as well since you could always exit the position by selling the LEAP to the market. If the underlying rises in price then you'll earn a small profit from the price appreciation as you would if you had owned the stock. The risk with this strategy is the same as it is with the regular covered call.

If the underlying stock decreases in price, then the LEAP premium will decrease and you'll be faced with a loss that the premium received from writing the short-term call will not compensate. As a result, our previous guidance with regards to managing this applies here as well.

Here's an example of how this strategy would work on the SPY, which is currently trading at $326.

Buy 1 deep ITM $288 call option on SPY expiring 6/30/2021 (334 days to expiry) for $46

Sell 1 slightly OTM $331 call option on SPY expiring 9/02/2020 (33 days to expiry) for $3.94

Difference between strikes = $43

Our upfront costs are ($43 + $3.94) - $46

Therefore our upfront premium is ($47.94 - $46) = $1.94 or $194

This means we need the cost to buy back our $331 call to drop below $0.94 for us to profit on the trade.

In terms of cash requirements, our single call options contract only costs us $4,600 to buy, as opposed to the $32,600 it would cost to buy 100 shares of SPY.

Volatility Advantages

The LEAP substitution offers an advantage in terms of handling volatility. This involves the way in which another Greek variable, Vega, affects the prices of LEAPs. Vega measures how an option's premium changes given a change in implied volatility.

LEAPs have their expiry dates far out into the future. Any increase in volatility produces a far greater rise in intrinsic value than it does in short-dated options. This means if the underlying starts rising, you'll realize a larger gain in the LEAP premium than you would by holding onto the stock itself. This works when the stock declines in price as well.

Since the LEAP is dated far out into the future, you could simply hold onto the position without fear of having to sell. Your LEAP won't lose too much of its premium since it still has immense time value present, even if it moves OTM. Of course, this won't help if the stock falls to zero, but if you follow the guidelines previously mentioned, this won't be a problem.

In terms of strike prices, you want your LEAP to finish ITM as much as possible, so look to buy options that have a delta greater than 0.75.

The previous advice regarding deltas closest to 0.4 applies to the short call.

Worst-Case Scenario

Let's say your trade isn't working out and the short-term option is moving ITM. In such a scenario, you need to cover your position and take the loss on it immediately. This is because if your option happens to get assigned to you, you'll need to have the cash on hand to be able to buy the stock.

You'll need to exercise the LEAP and deliver the stock to the short option's buyer. The primary reason for following this strategy is that you don't have the necessary cash to execute a traditional covered call. Therefore, it's unlikely you'll have the cash on hand to buy the underlying.

If you do choose to execute this strategy, our point is that be very vigilant of the short call moving ITM. If you're assigned the stock, it's far more disastrous for you than in the case of the traditional covered call. It might be worth it to write options even further OTM to prevent any chance of this scenario occurring.

Your broker may even automatically exercise your LEAP for you. If you don't have the cash on hand, you'll be hit with a margin call, and this is a scenario you want to avoid at all costs. This makes trade management even more important while your position is active.

THE TAX IMPLICATIONS OF THIS STRATEGY

Taxes are something that no investor can avoid. When it comes to covered calls, taxation can get a bit complex. We must mention at this point that we're not tax professionals. It's best for you to consult one if you're looking to figure your taxes out. The information in this chapter comes entirely from the Options Industry Council, which publishes tax information on the CBOE's website. Options taxation regulations keep changing, so it's best to consult with a tax professional at all times.

According to the Options Industry Council, profits from covered calls are treated as capital gains, with a few exceptions. We'll get to these exceptions shortly. The premium you earn by writing a call is a short-term capital gain and is taxed accordingly. Short-term capital gains are taxed at the same rates as ordinary income.

Gains and losses can be realized from the sale of the stock, from the call or from any combination of the two. If the stock is sold at a higher price than what it was bought for, this is a capital gain. Your holding period will determine whether this is a long-term or short-term capital gain. If you've been investing for a while now, you'll know that long-term capital gains result in lower tax rates.

In case the call is sold, a gain is realized when you cover your position (buy it back for a lower price than the premium you received on writing it). A capital loss is realized when you buy it back for a higher price than the premium you received. In the case that the call is assigned, the net profit or loss is taken into account and is taxed accordingly.

The dividends you earn while holding the stock might also be affected. This can get complicated, so it's best to consult with a tax professional who can walk you through the different scenarios affecting dividends.

As far as the IRS is concerned, the money you receive from selling a covered call is not included in your income upon writing. Instead, it is recognized when the call is closed. The call can close either by expiring worthless or by closing the position by buying it back. Being assigned is also a case where the call is considered closed.

Something to note is that the cash received at the time of the sale is a short-term capital gain irrespective of how long the short position was open. This is something investors miss. Even if you hold onto the short option for more than a year, the IRS will treat it as a short-term gain and tax you accordingly.

In the case of assignation, the strike price plus premium received equals the sale price of the stock when determining the gain or loss (*What Are The Tax Implications of Covered Calls?*, 2020). If the stock was held for a period greater than a year, the gain is treated as a long-term capital gain. The same applies for a loss.

Qualified Covered Calls

A covered call is considered qualified if it has more than 30 days to expiry when written and has a strike price that is not deep in the money. The exact quantification of deep in the money is subjective. The stock price is taken into account, as is the time left until expiry. The IRS is very subjective when it comes to this, so do consult a tax professional to understand the implications of this.

What does a covered call "qualify" for anyway? To understand this we need to look at how straddles are taxed. A straddle is a trade setup which we previously discussed. The nature of the trade makes its tax treatment complex and the IRS is concerned with investors using the losses from the strategy to offset capital gains before the latter have been recognized.

The good news is that as long as you write OTM calls, you don't need to worry about tax straddle rules. If you write ITM calls, you'll need to consult with a professional to determine your liability.

Qualified covered calls also impact the holding period of the underlying stock. This is best illustrated by an example. Let's say you buy 100 shares of a company for $100 in September. A month later the stock price declines to $80. You write a $79 call on the stock. This is considered an ITM qualified covered call as per IRS rules since it isn't deep ITM.

You then close the call position by buying it back for some price. Two days later, let's say the stock goes ex-dividend and you receive a dividend payment. You then sell the stock the following month. Here's how taxation will work in this scenario.

First, your dividend payment will not be treated as being qualified under any circumstances. With respect to dividends, qualified ones are taxed at long-term capital gains rates. In this case you did not hold the stock for 61 days during the prior 121-day holding period before the dividend was paid. Therefore, you'll pay ordinary income taxes on this payment.

Your total holding period was around two months (slightly less than 60 days). However, the period during which you held the ITM call will be subtracted from this since it is a qualified call. In this particular scenario, it doesn't affect your taxation rate. However, imagine a scenario where you hold a qualified ITM call for 90 days and the stock for 400 days and then sell the stock.

Your stock leg will be taxed at the short-term capital gains tax rate since your effective holding period will be (400 - 90) 310 days. If you had written an OTM call, the stock holding period will be 400. This impacts your dividend taxation as well. The number of days for which you hold the ITM call detracts from the necessary holding period to qualify for lower dividend taxation rates.

However, writing OTM calls doesn't reduce your tax liability. If anything, it complicates it. This is because such positions will be subject to tax straddle rules. If a non-qualified covered call is written on a stock position that is held for less than a year, the holding period for the stock is reduced by the period of time for which the call is held.

If the stock and option are closed at the same time, the gains are treated as short-term. If the call is closed first, the holding period for the stock resumes from the day the call was closed. These rules apply upon assignment as well. When calculating the gains and the appropriate tax rate, you need to take the holding period of the stock into account.

As long as your calls aren't deep ITM, your stock holding period will not decrease or be reduced. If the covered call isn't qualified, then your stock holding period will reduce and you'll end up paying the appropriate tax rate based on the shortened holding period.

The good news is that if you're writing options in an IRA, then you don't need to worry about any of this stuff. However, as we've mentioned earlier, you should not be using the money in your IRA to jeopardize long-term stock holdings. If you do choose this option, do so wisely, with conservative OTM strikes. If you wish to exit a position, then you need to line up another potential investment instead of letting cash lie dormant in your account.

THE BOTTOM LINE

Covered call taxation hinges mostly upon the strike price of your call. If it's deep ITM, then you're potentially creating a short-term capital gains tax situation for yourself. If you're looking to exit a sideways-moving stock position, make sure you've held onto the stock for at least a year before looking to let it go. This way the ITM call won't affect your holding period.

Consult a tax professional to determine which strikes would put you past the threshold of being qualified. If this is the case, you'll need to take higher short-term taxes into account when calculating the overall profit of your strategy. Dividends are also affected thanks to qualified/non-qualified covered calls due to the 61 day holding rule.

We also recommend you read all about options taxation at the CBOE's website. It might not be the most exciting thing you do today, but it is something which will save you future headaches.

You can access the relevant file at this link:

https://freemanpublications.com/optiontaxes

17

SETTING YOURSELF UP FOR SUCCESS

I t's one thing to read this book, but it's entirely another to achieve success in the markets. This is because executing a method well depends on your mindset and on your preparation. Many traders and investors think that making money in the markets is as simple as learning a strategy and then setting it up on autopilot.

This is not the case. We could provide two people with the same strategy and see one do well and the other fail to implement it. Mindset and the way you approach execution is extremely important. This is why $20,000 trading seminars exist after all. Many people attend such seminars but don't make any progress. Why is this?

THE PROBLEM WITH HOW MOST PEOPLE SET GOALS - AND HOW TO FIX IT

Goal setting is something everyone should do if they wish to get anywhere in life. The problem is that most of us aren't taught how to set goals. We invariably set goals that are measured by outside factors and influences. A typical financial goal is to "become a millionaire" or "to earn $10,000 per week" or something of this kind.

These goals are worthy, but they're not very helpful. For example, if you earned $9,000 in a given week, you've done incredibly well for yourself. However, this falls short of the $10,000 mark, so your subconscious mind knows you've failed. Many people face such situations and don't handle them well. They seek revenge on the markets and start chasing new systems that will "guarantee" $10,000 per week. This starts a downward spiral that most never recover from, which explains why so many people have a bad relationship with the stock market.

The solution to this is to change your goals instead. So which kinds of goals make the most sense? To understand this, we need to examine the nature of the market itself.

The market is a chaotic place. Over the long term, prices are driven by business quality and economic factors. However, in the short term, prices are driven by emotions.

There are methods of measuring all of these things, but you don't control anything when it comes to prices at the end of the day. You could have invested in a great business with great management, but the stock prices could remain firmly in place no matter how great the company is.

You could scream and shout at how irrational the market is, but the market is going to do whatever it wants. Attaching the success or failure of your goals to such an erratic thing doesn't make sense. Instead, you need to figure out what your processes are and attach your goals to them. This way, you'll always make progress since progress becomes as simple as doing something.

Let's look at an example of something that many people try to accomplish but fail: Losing weight and getting fit. The most common goal statement to achieve this is along the lines of "I will lose 10lbs in two months". The problem with this statement is that while it's fully measurable and time-bound, it isn't within your control. You could drink too much water one day and end up losing just nine pounds. Does this mean you've failed?

Instead of creating outcome orientated goals, how about creating process-oriented goals? Take a look at the list below:

- Exercise for one hour 5x per week, either in the gym or through another activity
- Be physically active as much as possible
- Walk instead of using transportation, where possible
- Prepare food ahead of time to prevent snacking
- Buy groceries to make sure healthy food is always in the kitchen
- Incorporate one cheat meal every week to relieve stress

None of these goals are out of your reach. All you need to do is take action. By taking action on these goals you'll automatically make progress. You won't be looking into the future, trying to figure out how much longer you have to go. You'll be in the present moment and be focused on doing what you need to do to get where you want to be.

The same principles ensure investment and trading success as well. A sample list of goals for a covered call writer would be:

- I will study 5 charts every weekday.
- I will always use the closest strike price to 0.4 delta when entering a trade.
- I will use a rules-based approach to exiting my trade.
- I will log every single trade in my trading journal.
- I will review my trades every week to see where I could improve.
- I will continue to paper trade while trading live to sharpen my sword. I will do this until I have at least 100 live trades under my belt.

All of these goals are completely within your control. Best of all, they don't depend on the amount of money you make to measure progress. In the markets, it's quite common to do all the right things and still lose money. For example, you could enter a position based on solid principles, but some unforeseen event, such as the Covid-19 pandemic, might occur and push your positions into negative territory.

Relying on results to define your goals only puts you in a position to lose your power. You'll never feel as if you're making progress doing this. How can you? You're trying to control something that cannot be controlled. Instead, always focus on what you can control. By doing this, you're stacking the deck for success.

Routines and Habits

Goal setting is one half of the success formula. The other half is a well-practiced routine that will ensure you meet with success. Most traders and investors have extremely unstructured routines when it comes to looking at the markets. The key to good performance is a structured method that is based on intelligent principles.

What a lot of unsuccessful market participants do is hear someone talking about some stock or investment idea, and they jump into it without considering its merits. They don't take the time to educate themselves on how these methods work. They don't pause to think whether this method would suit them or not.

Instead, they let promises cloud their judgment. Investors don't need to be all that active when it comes to the market. They need to put in the work upfront and then sit back and monitor their investments for validity.

When you begin involving options, your day-to-day routines are of greater importance. You cannot afford to roll out of bed on a poor night's sleep and then sit down to trade. This will only cause you to lose money. Before placing a trade or an investment, conduct a quick check of yourself. Are you a little too emotional right now? Are you making this decision from a place of rationality, or are you gambling? Where is this decision coming from?

Can you explain this investment idea in plain and simple words to someone who has no idea about it? Only when you receive suitable answers to all of these questions should you put your money into the market. If you're a trader, then instill habits that you can execute repeatedly and consistently. If you find that your routine is being disturbed, then don't trade that day.

Also, your routine after you've finished trading matters as well. As we mentioned earlier, the markets are random. At times, you will receive poor results despite doing everything correctly. This doesn't mean you're a bad trader or that you lack skills. It's just how the markets work. Conduct a thorough review of your actions, including your mental state, and remind yourself of all the good things you did. If you did some things that conflicted with your routines, make sure you don't do them again by removing the things that triggered them.

Focus on taking action and on instilling the right habits, and you'll meet with success for sure. The key is to aim for incremental success over time. Most people try to go ahead and achieve everything at once, which is impractical. What most often happens is that they end up burning themselves out and they find themselves right back at square one.

With regards to covered calls, don't try to place too many trades at once. Place one at first and see how you do. Then add another and so on until you reach a number you're comfortable with. Track your habits and processes, and over time you'll end up reaching where you want to be.

18

A PASSIVE INCOME STRATEGY
WITH COVERED CALL FUNDS

T he financial markets can be taken advantage of through many different strategies. All of these strategies are implemented by managed funds such as mutual funds or exchange traded funds (ETFs). You can passively adopt these strategies by buying units of such funds and pay a management fee in return. Covered calls are no exception to this.

Commonly, covered call funds carry the label "enhanced equity" in their names and these funds seek to generate returns by combining dividend investment with covered call writing. The aim of these funds is to beat the S&P 500 and to minimize the tax bill that investors face.

There is also another set of funds called closed-end funds (CEFs) that aim to achieve the same objective. Closed-end funds are an interesting breed of funds in that unlike mutual funds, they don't issue new units. Instead, the only units you can buy are from other investors in the fund. For this reason, you'll sometimes end up paying a premium to the funds' net asset values (NAV) when buying units.

Despite this phenomenon, closed-end funds don't provide the average investor with too much of an advantage. The average closed-end fund charges fees to the order of one percent of capital invested. This is the same as what a hedge fund charges its investors. As such, you're better off investing in an ETF since their fees tend to be lower.

The exception to this rule is if the CEF is trading at a discount to its net asset value. This happens from time to time, and is a useful way to offset the fund's management fee. You can screen for funds currently trading at a discount using the following website

https://www.cefchannel.com/screens/discount-to-nav/

ADVANTAGES OF COVERED CALL FUNDS

There are many advantages of investing in managed funds. Many people don't have the time, nor the desire to actively monitor their investments, and this is why passive investing strategies exist in the first place. Covered calls aren't exactly an active strategy, but you do need to be aware of what the market is doing. They also need to be up to speed with price behavior.

In some cases, a tiny dash of technical analysis might also be necessary to make sense of an investment. All of this puts additional strain on the investor, and some people might not want to take this workload on. In such cases, it makes sense to outsource money management to a professional manager who can optimize a portfolio to bring maximum benefit to an investor.

These managers will search for the best opportunities in the market and will employ an active approach to writing covered calls. Thus, the potential returns you can earn are quite high.

Lower Investment

When reviewing the poor man's covered call strategy, we hit upon one particular snag that might stop you from writing covered calls: a lack of money. If implementing covered calls using LEAPs isn't for you, you could turn to a managed covered call fund such as Blackrock Enhanced Equity Dividend Trust (BDJ).

This currently trades at $7.50, and there is no minimum investment required. It has an expense ratio of 0.8% and is actively traded with a good amount of liquidity. The fund is issued by Blackrock, which is a highly respected firm in the investment arena. This is a cheap and easy way for you to enter the field of covered call writing.

Optimization

Long-term investors will benefit from investing in covered call funds as well. If you were to implement covered calls by yourself, you would adopt a purely passive strategy. However, there are many ways to make an active covered call strategy work. These strategies seek to earn profits on both the stock as well as the option leg of the trade.

This is the approach these funds take. If you're looking to give your portfolio a little boost, then investing in such funds might make sense for you. Optimization also appears in the form of tax advantages. These funds seek to capture dividends as well as seek to minimize the tax bill you will face.

Monitoring all of this is a headache if you're an individual. It takes time and effort. Instead, pay a small fee and have your money managed for you.

DISADVANTAGES

Covered call funds offer good opportunities, but there are some drawbacks. For starters, they seek to outperform the market, and like most mutual funds with similar aims, most of them fail to achieve this goal. Market outperformance is not an easy thing to achieve, and in many cases, it's far easier to shoot for average gains instead of trying to beat the market.

These funds also experience volatility thanks to a few of their trades going the wrong way. While a well-managed fund will keep any adverse impact in check, it doesn't change the market's view of them. As a result, they tend to underperform in good times and perform worse in bad times. This is because in good times, investors rush into index funds, and in bad times, the market identifies these covered call funds as being historical underperformers and punishes them.

If you're willing to stomach a few ups and downs, then covered call funds might offer benefits for you. However, you need to hold on tight. The other disadvantage is that their fees are higher than the average index fund and ETF. Index funds and ETFs can charge fees as low as 0.03%.

Compare that to the 0.8% mentioned earlier, and you'll see the difference. These fees pose a higher hurdle for the investor to overcome, and given the historic volatility inherent in these funds, it might not be worth the risk. Our advice is that if you have the time to monitor your covered calls, then write them yourself.

A covered call doesn't require much maintenance. It takes just a few minutes to identify an optimal strike price and determine how much of a premium you want to get paid. Manage it yourself, and you won't have to pay any fees.

If you're looking to be more active as an investor, then simply buying shares in a fund is counter to your objective. After all, the point of being active is to generate more money than the market. If you cannot do this by yourself, then there's no point in investing in a fund that tries to do the same.

19

AVOIDING TRADING SCAMS

Options trading and indeed trading, in general, has acquired a "get-rich-quick" taint. As a result, there are many operators out there who promise you all the money in the world with their super-secret trading systems. All you have to do is pay their hefty fee. These self-appointed gurus can be found on YouTube and Twitter posting screenshots of 1,000% gains thanks to their simple strategies.

It's easy to fall for such scams since the people behind them are often excellent salespeople. They make various claims that are designed to convince you that you cannot do any of this by yourself and that you need their guidance to profit. They might even claim to have worked at some hedge fund or have started their own hedge fund before deciding to shutter it.

It's pretty easy to fall for such claims, so we'll now give you a list of the telltale signs that all of these scam artists exhibit. Use this checklist to avoid them.

GET RICH QUICK. REALLY QUICK.

This is the most obvious sign, and truth be told, it functions as a filter for the fake guru. People who are desperate to make loads of money fall for scams because they want to believe such claims are true. The most common claim is that the trader in question turned $1,000 into $1,000,000 in the matter of a year by trading options.

Please note that there have been traders who have turned small amounts of money into enormous amounts in the past. For example, the pioneer of computerized trading, Ed Seykota turned $5,000 into $15 million in 12 years, and commodities trader Michael Marcus turned $30,000 into $80 million in 15 years. These are extraordinary returns that are well beyond the norm.

However, the fake guru will claim such returns in the space of a single year or two years at the most. They'll tell you they started off in poverty and used trading to gain access to a life of helicopters and champagne. They'll even post videos of them in a bathrobe at their Ritz-Carlton penthouse suite. The markets have the ability to make you rich, but it's close to impossible to earn such massive returns in such a short period of time without assuming huge amounts of risk.

LEVERAGE

One of the ways that these scammers justify such large returns is through the use of leverage. They'll regularly highlight that they use 100x leverage on their trades and that this is the only way for you to make money. This is a bit like a real estate guru who claims to have a multimillion dollar real estate empire, but really has only has millions of dollars worth of mortgages on their balance sheet.

Just like how you need to stay away from companies that utilize a ton of debt to boost returns, you need to steer clear of traders who use excessive leverage to boost returns. This phenomenon is well-known in the institutional trading industry. For this reason, traders pay attention to risk-adjusted returns instead of outright returns.

The best metric for this is the Sharpe Ratio. This number takes the leverage used into account and presents a good picture of how skillful a trader really is. A Sharpe Ratio greater than one is considered pretty good. Risk-adjusted return metrics such as these can help you differentiate between a trader who risks 100% of their capital to generate 30% returns versus another that risks just 2% of their capital to generate 15% returns. It's pretty obvious who the better trader is in this case.

NO AUDITED RECORDS

It's straightforward to establish an audit trail for your trading records. Even if you're a retail trader, it's as simple as downloading them directly from your broker software or website. However, this is an extremely tough task for most fake trading gurus. They'll do their absolute best not to disclose their trading account balances or their trade histories.

They'll provide all kinds of excuses that their broker doesn't connect to online auditing platforms or that they have too much money in their accounts, and they're afraid this might make them a target. This argument is a bit odd since the very premise of getting you to sign up with them is that they make a lot of money.

Some gurus are aware of this dichotomy and post screenshots of trades on Twitter and YouTube. However, they'll obscure whether this account was a demo account or a live one. They won't disclose the account number or the account balance, so you won't have any way of knowing whether this example was chosen in retrospect or in real-time. Some gurus even use market simulation software to replay the market and then present it as a real-time trade.

The easiest way to spot such scammers is to ask them what their Sharpe Ratio is. If they cannot give you this number, run away from them. Every professional trader knows this number by heart. It's how they're evaluated at the end of the day.

Another branch of audits concerns the fake hedge fund gurus. The phrase hedge fund is tossed around very quickly these days because most retail traders have no idea how a hedge fund works. A "hedge fund" can be a single person with a Bloomberg terminal shacked up in their garage, or it can be a financial behemoth with 1,500 employees headquartered in a multi-million dollar skyscraper in Manhattan.

Whatever the situation is, anyone operating a hedge fund needs to have a license from the SEC. This securities-dealing license needs to be renewed periodically, and anyone who has traded for an institution possesses one. Ask the scam artist to show you their securities-dealing license. Pay attention to the type of licenses as well.

You can even check the validity of their license on the Financial Regulatory Authority's website (https://www.finra.org/investors/protect-your-money/ask-and-check). No excuse is a valid explanation for not having a FINRA or SEC license. If they claim to have run or traded for a hedge fund, they need to possess one of these, even if it's expired.

Ask them which broker-dealer they traded through. Hedge funds cannot trade through regular brokers since the compliance requirements are different. They need to trade through so-called Prime Brokers. These brokers are the ones that hold their license certifications and monitor them for any violations.

If a guru promises you an offer where your trades can be routed to certain brokers in their network, ask to see their broker-dealer agreement. If there is no agreement, the guru is probably bucketing your orders and is trading against you. In this scam, what happens is that your orders (along with the other students') are grouped together, and the guru then takes the opposite side of those trades.

Most moves lose money, so it makes sense to teach students some bogus system and then trade against them. Over the long run, the scammer will make money. You'll see this happen quite a lot in the world of Forex trading. So always ask for official documents and double-check their validity as much as possible. Excuses or simple screenshots which show no identifying information are not good enough.

GIMMICKS

Gurus usually push their strategies as being super-secret. They may even make you sign an NDA before enrolling in their program. You'll see a very active blog with comments mentioning how amazing their system is. The same goes for their YouTube channels and other social media. Needless to say, many of these comments are fake.

Ethel McKeown 3 weeks ago

Bitcoin's halving is now in the past, and stock-to-flow formulas predict that the asset is ready to rocket out from current lows. But that's yet to happen, and the crypto market is even crashing currently. this why it's advisable to trade with the help of expert traders like Kevin Mccarthy He is always one step ahead of other traders, he fully monitored all my trades to avoid me making mistakes and losing my money. My earnings have increased drastically from 1.2 Bitcoin to 6 Bitcoin in just 4 weeks and some days. I have full confidence in his tradin abilities. You all can reach out to him through [<< Tele-grm >> Mccarthytrade

Figure 17: An example of a fake guru testimonial posted on a YouTube video. Tell tales signs of fakery are: Using an American name but typing in broken English, mentioning the guru by name (in this case, one "Kevin McCarthy"), claiming they made huge amounts of money in a short time, and advertising the guru's Telegram channel or WhatsApp number

There is no secret formula or information that anyone is hiding from you. It's all there in plain sight. The problem isn't with the information, it's with the way you expect to run your trading operations. If you expect to get rich quick, nothing is going to work for you. Aim to get rich slowly, and you'll be surprised at how friendly the markets are in terms of making money.

Here's a simple checklist for you to follow when evaluating a trading guru:

1. Conduct proper research about the trading service and compare it with its peers. Take special note of the refund policy; many of these scam services do not even have one.
2. Investigate whether the service you are considering is regulated by the SEC.
3. Learn the basics of the stock market by reading entry level books like William O'Neill's *How to Make Money in Stocks* or our own *8 Step Beginner's Guide to Value Investing* before subscribing to any service.
4. Carefully read all the terms and conditions.
5. Consider online and offline reviews on an unbiased website like Trustpilot.
6. And finally, make sure the company is 100% transparent in their fees and policies.

We must note that courses offered by trading gurus don't fall under the purview of the SEC or FINRA. Use online review sites and the previous tips mentioned to avoid scam artists.

FREEMAN COVERED CALL RULE #15

DO YOUR DUE DILIGENCE BEFORE SIGNING UP TO ANY TRADING SERVICE

WHERE YOU GO FROM HERE

The final question this all boils down to is, do you want to make your existing investments work for you?

We've discussed asymmetric returns and how the market trades (both the total index as well as individual stocks) flat the majority of the time. This is what makes covered calls such a great way for you to generate additional income in your stock portfolio.

There are two ways to approach it. You could use them as a generator of synthetic dividends on your long stock holdings, or you could use them as a speculative strategy where you can try to capture the gains from the stock leg as well as the option premium. If you can generate an additional two to three percent over and above any dividends you're earning in your long stock portfolio; you're giving yourself an extra gain of five percent per year.

Once this amount is reinvested and compounded, you'll end up doubling your money over your holding period when compared to generating no income from it. Many investors discount the power of cash flow, and we hope this book has opened your eyes to how powerful it can truly be for your portfolio.

Covered calls aren't a silver bullet. You need to follow some simple principles to make sure they work for you. You need to take note of the deltas of the options you write. Stick to writing options with a delta of 0.4 as much as possible, and you'll be just fine. If you're writing calls for investment purposes, then sticking to lower delta values makes more sense. Your premiums will be lower, but you won't be in any danger of losing your long stock position.

When prices are increasing massively, you're probably better off only buying the stock and then writing far OTM calls against it instead of earning a premium by writing a put and waiting for it to fall, which might never happen. The capital gains you give up will far outweigh whatever premiums you earn from the put.

This is why covered calls are best written when the market is moving sideways or slightly upwards. If you're in it for investment purposes, then pretty much any condition will work for you except a wildly bullish one. If you're in it for speculative purposes, then you need to avoid bearish markets. The capital losses on your stock leg will outweigh the premiums you earn.

You could roll your options down and reduce your cost basis, but there's no guarantee that you'll ever be able to overcome the capital loss. You'll also need to carefully choose your rolled strikes since you don't want to inadvertently take a loss on the stock leg.

Despite all of these factors, covered calls are a simple income strategy. The only instance in which they turn complex is when you deal with taxation. We've covered this in detail but still advise you to consult a tax professional, especially with regards to writing ITM calls.

Beware of any scammers and use the tips we've given you to steer clear of them. Before jumping into covered calls, take some time to note your gains and losses on paper. This way you'll reduce your downside risk.

Many ordinary investors have grown their financial portfolio by using covered calls in addition to their long stock holdings. That's the beauty of them, because you can profit even when the stock is going nowhere. When used smartly and in moderation, options transform from a gambling tool, to an intelligent investor's best friend.

With the rise in discount brokers, and affordable access to great information, there has simply never been a better time to be an investor, so you should feel thankful that you're living in the times you are.

To demonstrate this, let's run some numbers one last time.

We'll take $25,000, and to that, we'll add $2,500 every year. At a compounded rate of 15% (10% from your long stock holdings + an additional 5% generated by covered calls).

At this rate, you can turn that $25,000 into $1 million in twenty three years.

Are you up for the challenge?

One final word from us. If this book has helped you in any way, we'd appreciate it if you left a review on Amazon. Reviews are the lifeblood of our business. We read every single one and incorporate your feedback into our future book projects.

To leave an Amazon review, scan the QR code below or go to
https://freemanpublications.com/leaveareview

"THE MOST SUCCESSFUL PEOPLE IN LIFE ARE THE ONES WHO ASK QUESTIONS. THEY'RE ALWAYS LEARNING. THEY'RE ALWAYS GROWING. THEY'RE ALWAYS PUSHING."

- Robert Kiyosaki

OTHER BOOKS BY FREEMAN PUBLICATIONS (AVAILABLE ON AMAZON & AUDIBLE)

You can learn more about our other titles by going to

https://freemanpublications.com/books

Or if you prefer listening you can find our Audiobooks at

https://freemanpublications.com/audiobooks

REFERENCES

Baird, J. (2007, September 28). How M&G played CDOs to profit during the crisis. *Reuters*. https://www.reuters.com/article/mg-crisis-cdos/how-mg-played-cdos-to-profit-during-the-crisis-idUSL2783735020070928

Belvedere, M. J. (2019, December 13). *How the Icahn-Ackman "Battle of the Billionaires" on CNBC became a defining moment of the decade*. CNBC. https://www.cnbc.com/2019/12/13/reliving-the-carl-icahn-and-bill-ackman-herbalife-feud-on-cnbc.html

Case Study - Warren Buffett Writing Put Options To Obtain A Lower Stock Purchase Price. (2019, May 20). The Options Manual. https://optionsmanual.com/secondary-informational-articles/case-study_-warren-buffet-writing-put-options-to-obtain-a-lower-stock-purchase-price/

Ferreira, J. (2019, April 10). *US Inflation Rate Rises Above Forecasts in March*. Tradingeconomics.Com; TRADING ECONOMICS. https://tradingeconomics.com/united-states/inflation-cpi

Graham, B., Buffett, W. E., & Zweig, J. (2013). *The intelligent investor: a book of practical counsel.* Harper Collins.

History of Options Trading - How Options Came About. (2017). Option-strading.Org. https://www.optionstrading.org/history/

Mackay, C. (2014). *Extraordinary popular delusions and the madness of crowds.* Maestro Reprints.

Nagarajan, shalini. (2020, May 1). *Bill Ackman turned a $27 million bet into $2.6 billion in a genius investment. Here are 12 of the best trades of all time. | Markets Insider.* Markets.Businessinsider.Com. https://markets.businessinsider.com/news/stocks/best-trades-of-all-time-big-short-soros-ackman-bass-2020-5-1029198259

Russel, J. (2009). *Prevent Losses in Your Forex Trading.* The Balance. https://www.thebalance.com/why-do-forex-traders-lose-money-1344936

Schatzker, E. (2020, May 7). *Bloomberg - Are you a robot?* Www.Bloomberg.Com. https://www.bloomberg.com/news/articles/2020-05-07/paul-tudor-jones-buys-bitcoin-says-he-s-reminded-of-gold-in-70s

Schroeder, A. (2009). *The snowball: Warren Buffett and the business of life.* Bantam Books.

Smith, S. (2019, May 15). *What Percentage of Options Expire Worthless?* Stocknews.Com. https://stocknews.com/what-percentage-of-options-explore-worthless-2019-05/

Wathen, J. (2013, November 16). *3 of Warren Buffett's Weirdest Invest-ments.* The Motley Fool. https://www.fool.com/investing/general/2013/11/16/3-of-warren-buffetts-weirdest-investments.aspx

What Are The Tax Implications of Covered Calls? (2020, January 20). Www.Fidelity.Com. https://www.fidelity.com/learning-center/investment-products/options/generating-income-with-covered-calls/tax-implications-covered-calls

Made in United States
Troutdale, OR
02/28/2024

18050168R00111